CHILDREN OF JONAH

Also by James T. Clemons

What Does the Bible Say about Suicide?
Minneapolis: Fortress Press, 1990; 2d ed., Nashville: Parthenon
Press

Perspectives on Suicide (editor and contributor)
Louisville: Westminster/John Knox, 1989

Sermons on Suicide (editor and contributor)
Louisville: Westminster/John Knox, 1990

CHILDREN OF JONAH

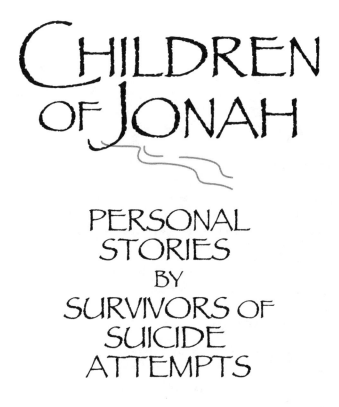

PERSONAL STORIES BY SURVIVORS OF SUICIDE ATTEMPTS

James T. Clemons, Editor

Foreword by Judy Collins

CAPITAL
BOOKS, INC.
Sterling, Virginia

Capital Books, Inc.
P.O. Box 605
Herndon, Virginia 20172-0605

ISBN 1-892123-54-1 (alk. paper)

Library of Congress Cataloging-in-Publication Data

Children of Jonah : personal stories by survivors of suicide attempts/
James T. Clemons, editor; foreword by Judy Collins.
      p. cm.
   ISBN 1-892123-54-1 (pbk.)
      1. Suicidal behavior—Biography. I. Clemons, James T.
   II. Collins, Judy, 1939–
   RC569 .C475 2001
   62.28–dc13   2001047051

Printed in Canada on acid-free paper that meets
the American National Standards Institute Z39-48 Standard.

First Edition

10 9 8 7 6 5 4 3 2 1

CONTENTS

Contents

FOREWORD

There is a Hebrew saying that if you can save one life, you can save the world. The life that is spared, that suicide might have taken, can perhaps be a kind of talisman to save others who might follow the tangled, unpredictable journey of the would-be suicide. A failed suicide, then, might save the world.

This is a book of true celebration, about the lives of people of all ages, many different walks of life, who have tried to take their own lives, going to the edge and coming back to report to us what it was like to survive and how they see the world, and their own lives, in a different light. We can rejoice that they, like soldiers on a dangerous mission, lived to tell us the tale of their exploits. They are, in their own lives, heroes and heroines, and have something to teach us.

Today, there are ten thousand suicide attempts each day in the United States alone. This statistic spells a plague of such immense proportions in terms of mental, physical, emotional, and spiritual health that it is hard to imagine. We must look, and listen, to the messages of pain and fear, hopelessness and despair that drive these disparate, and desperate, individuals to try to take their own lives. It is said that most of these attempts are cries for help, and that no attempt is halfhearted, that all are serious and should be taken as such.

And all suicide attempts have at least some chance of leading to death.

Every year, over thirty thousand in the United States succeed in their suicide attempts, and for each person who succeeds, it is said that an average of ten people must suffer the pain of being suicide survivors.

A failed suicide could have saved my world. My son took his own life, plummeting mine into the search for an answer to the unanswerable questions that suicide raises. My own failure at killing myself when I was fourteen saved my world, and the world of my father and mother, who, I think, could not have survived the death of their oldest child.

Suicide is alluring, compelling, seductive, driven by chemical dependency, mental illness, depression, fear. In many times and cultures in history, it has been considered illegal. Alfred Alvarez, in his book *The Savage God*,[1] tells of a man who was hanged for unsuccessfully trying to kill himself by slitting his throat. Alvarez also calls a suicide a "closed world with it own irresistible logic." For those of us who have gone there and come back from the edge of the precipice, it is also the great mystery. Why others and not us? Why did a friend of mine try twenty-five times to take her own life when she was drinking, never try again when she was sober, and why did my son, who was drinking at the time, succeed in taking his own life on his third try?

With suicide there is also always the question of the power and the honor of choice. If I don't have the choice to select the time when I depart this life, I have no real personal freedom at the root of self-determination. I have the right, if I choose, to end my life. The problem with most of us who are young and healthy in most

1. Alfred Alvarez, *The Savage God* (New York: Random House, 1972).

respects except mental illness and addiction and the depression disease, is that we don't really choose. The substance chooses for us, perhaps alcohol or drugs, legal and illegal; or the untreated depression chooses. We don't choose, in most cases, though we would like to think we do. Often, our self-determination is an illusion. Other forces, powerful, seductive, negative, and often treatable with therapy as well as the new antidepressant drugs, are in control.

The stories in this remarkable collection are told by people who could be our children, our sisters, brothers, friends, many of whom may have lent great beauty to their families and their worlds, and then taken us on the journey into what Camus called the one truly serious philosophical problem.

For centuries, suicides have had to deal with the condemnation of the church and state. Only recently have insurance companies started to pay out on policies after a suicide. The church has in recent years softened its stance on suicide. After the death of my son, a woman whose father had been a Catholic shared with me that, when her father had taken his own life, the priest told her mother that her husband could be buried in the cemetery, but he would not be borne in the hearse through the gate, in the customary manner. Instead he would be carried into the cemetery in his casket over closed gates. The image stayed with me as though seared into my brain.

Another survivor of a parent's death when she was seven or eight admitted that, when her father died, his name was simply never mentioned again in her family, until the time she herself was in her forties. Even his tombstone did not bear his name. When she was an adult, in her forties, she began the painful work of remembering, naming, and mourning her long-dead father.

Survivors must often bear such pain and indignity, and often, the memory of the loved one, the one who has gone by way of his or her own hand, is layered over with mystery and myth, sorrow and un-kindness, misunderstanding, and, often, unintentional, even calcu-lated cruelty. As a survivor, I swore that I would try to break those bonds of the taboo and speak out for myself and for my son, as well as for other survivors of this sorrowful loss.

Having experienced my own suicide attempt at the age of four-teen, I have always had respect and awe for the powerful impulses that drive many of us to try to take our own lives. I went into therapy in my early twenties, and there were many years when I was drinking that the lure of the "big drink," that moment when suicide appears to be the only way out, drew me into the darkness. I have experi-enced a great deal of depression in my life, and for many years at-tempted to control my suicidal urges with alcohol as well as with other drugs. For me, the solution to my suicidal thinking has been a spiritual journey, which has involved becoming sober and changing my negative habits of thinking, as well as using exercise and positive support groups to guide me from those deadly thoughts. I respect the demon, and only grace has kept him at bay in my own life. I do not go there, a day at a time.

As the survivor of my son's suicide, I have been through the terri-ble grief that comes with losing a beloved child as well as a beautiful spirit in my life and in the lives of my family. I know, too, that I have not been singled out for pain and loss. There are all kinds of tragedy and loss in people's lives. But I think suicide is different, and it is important to put the taboos to rest finally, to relinquish our punishment of the suicide and his or her family, and realize that un-derstanding, compassion, and medical treatment in the form of therapies and appropriate drugs are the way of knowledge and must be applied to the treatment of this disease—for it is a disease, the depression disease, that leads to the urge to take one's own life.

Much of my healing after my son's death took place when others shared their stories with me. This is a book especially for the wounded, which most of us are. These stories moved me and helped me understand, on a deeper level, some of what many must go through to live. I know they will help your journey.

The book is filled with powerful testimony. Each story is unique, yet links us in the shared mystery of survival. The mystics, poets, and philosophers tell us that only the heart speaks to the heart.

The hearts in these stories speak to our hearts.

—Copyright 2001 Judy Collins/
The Wildflower Co.

INTRODUCTION:
Take Me and Throw Me
Into the Sea

Jonah, the ancient prophet of Hebrew Scripture, was only one among many across the ages who asked to die, who tried to end his life, but went on to accomplish worthwhile things for others.

> *Take me and throw me into the sea;*
> *then the sea will quiet down for you;*
> *for I know it is because of me*
> *that this great storm has come upon you.*

Elie Wiesel, survivor of the Holocaust, author, and recipient of the 1986 Nobel Peace Prize, included Jonah in his small volume, *Five Biblical Portraits*.[1] In his view, Jonah was unlucky, the quintessential antihero, with a taste for failure and tragedy and a "peculiar combination of life force and death wish." He underscored Jonah's suicidal behavior and speech.

While reviewing biblical and other ancient texts for *What Does the Bible Say about Suicide?* and without having read Wiesel's book at

1. Elie Wiesel, *Five Biblical Portraits* (South Bend, Ind.: Univ. of Notre Dame Press, 1981).

the time, I became convinced that Jonah, besides having other behavioral and theological problems, was not only suicidal but also a
survivor of a suicide attempt.[2] This was according to the definition I
had adopted before beginning my research: Suicide is the choice and
successful completion of the act to end one's life, regardless of motive, circumstance, or method.

At the end of my discussion of Jonah, I suggested that, if ever those
who have attempted suicide should form a group, they might well
choose the name Children of Jonah. For they, like him, have survived an attempt and received a second chance. Perhaps, like him,
they have gone on to do significant things for others, maybe without
even knowing it. And certainly like him, they have plumbed the
depths of human experience and been confronted by some of life's
most profound questions.

My book was first published more than a decade ago. At the time,
I had no thought that I would ever be editing a book of personal stories by those who had survived such an experience, or, as I now envi-
sion, helping to create an organization for them. With the founding
of the Organization of Attempters and Survivors of Suicide in Interfaith Services (OASSIS) in 1997, however, and after a year of con-
sultation with leaders in different fields, I decided to explore both
possibilities. I first helped start an organization for survivors of suicide attempts, then began work on this book.

As I sought the opinions of leading suicidologists about the need
for a collection of accounts like these, some questioned whether
those who had attempted to take their own lives would be willing to
have their stories appear in print. That concern prompted my mo-
mentary consideration that we might have to make an appeal over

2. James T. Clemons, *What Does the Bible Say about Suicide?* (Minneapolis,
Minn.: Fortress Press; 1990; 2d ed., Nashville, Tenn.: Parthenon Press, 1990).

the World Wide Web. Within a few weeks, however, I had thought of a few people whom I might ask to contribute and was very pleased with their immediate willingness to do so, which strongly suggested that many other survivors of attempted suicide might also be willing to share their stories. And so the collection began.

Exploring the Dark Terrain

The inner world of survivors of suicide attempts can best be known only to those who have experienced it. Despite their own enormous suffering, family and friends, regardless of how close, can catch but brief and shallow glimpses of the survivors' intense pain, self-doubt, ethical probing, and theological questioning. The best-trained therapists realize certain dynamics and, by prescribing the proper medication, have helped thousands who are depressed and who are also suicidal to find meaningful, happy lives. But most caregivers can hardly pretend to know all that is "going on" in their clients' minds. Often they are shocked to learn of the end of a meaningful relationship with someone they have tried to help.

Judith F. Meade is a therapist and cofounder of Therapy Professionals at Tyson's Corner in Northern Virginia. Not long after she began her practice, she lost a client to suicide. "My worst fear became a reality." She was not alone.

A 1993 poll showed that 97 percent of clinicians were afraid of losing a client in this way. Meade later wrote that when the call came, she felt "numbness, shock, denial, guilt, fear, shame, and anxiety." After working closely with other clinicians, she helped form, and was asked to chair, a Clinician Survivors Committee within the American Association of Suicidology.

Therapists generally agree that no suicide occurs as the result of a single cause. Researchers and analysts who perform psychological "autopsies" of suicides usually find a tangled web of cause and effect that must be painstakingly unraveled in order to gain insights that will provide clues for prevention. But it is the survivors of attempts themselves who are best able to reveal their often mysterious and inexplicable thoughts, along with their indomitable stamina, in spite of overwhelming depression, loss of self-image, shame, and the will to live. They bring insights into that inner world unavailable anywhere else. Indeed, they lead us into one of the darkest terrains of human experience.

Children of Jonah offers a unique collection of deeply emotional stories by these survivors, in their own words—raw, unreserved, scary. Yet they move us from illness, through insight and understanding, to self-acceptance and hope.

A Look at the Numbers

To understand the importance of this book, we must see it in terms of the number of people who actually seek to end their lives and the consequences of their acts both for those closest to them and, in a broader sense, for society.

Suicide now claims the lives of one million people a year worldwide, more than 30,000 a year in the United States—one every seventeen minutes.

Karen Marshall, Founding Chair of the London County Suicide Prevention Coalition in Northern Virginia, lost her father and an uncle to suicide. She often uses a graphic illustration. What would we do if every day of the year a plane with eighty-three people fell from the skies killing everyone on board?

For every two homicides in America, there are three suicides. Many know that the highest suicide rates are among the elderly. Few realize that the Bureau of Health Statistics begins its categories of suicide at age five.

Against these statistics of completed suicide, the numbers of attempted suicides are even more shocking and tragic. According to the U.S. Surgeon General's *Call to Action to Prevent Suicide*, "each year in the United States, approximately 500,000 people require emergency room treatment as a result of attempted suicide."[3]

At the Surgeon General's Press Conference in Washington, D.C., on May 2, 2001, the *National Strategy for Suicide Prevention: Goals and Objectives for Action* was released; it put the number of people attempting suicide at 650,000 annually.

On the same day, the National Association of Mental Illness announced the startling new results of a survey they had requested from Roper Starch Worldwide, Inc. It indicated that as many as 8.4 million American adults, 4 percent of those eighteen and older, have contemplated suicide. More than 6.3 million American adults have had continuing "thoughts of suicide throughout the same two-week period." High school students have a very high rate of suicidal ideation.

A Call for Help

These statistics in themselves call for specific attention to a group of people too long neglected, too long misunderstood, and too long left alone to carry their own burdens. The stigma and op-

3. U.S. Surgeon General, *Call to Action to Prevent Suicide* (Washington, D.C.: Dept. of Health and Human Services, U.S. Public Health Service, Washington, D.C., 1999).

pression they endure from their friends, their religious communities, and even their families arise from a society still influenced by centuries of harsh, shameful teachings. Thus they are often cut off from those most able to help and from those to whom they would normally turn for compassion and support.

Survivors of suicide attempts are at a very high risk to complete the act. Previous attempts are one of the two major common factors in the "anatomy" of suicides, the second being untreated depression. Thus each attempt, however slight, however "experimental" or "attention-getting" it may seem, must be taken seriously by the attempter, those closest to them, and certainly by their therapists and medical advisers.

We hear frequently of survivors of a suicide, far less about survivors of suicide attempts. In planning for the First National Interfaith Conference on Religion and Suicide in Atlanta in April 2000, OASSIS invited Ken Tullis to be on its panel of four survivors of attempted suicide. Other presenters were Meri Nana-Ama Danquah, author of *Willow Weep for Me* and DeQuincy Lezine, advocate for suicide prevention from an attempter's perspective.[4]

Tullis's immediate response was, "I'll come, if Madge can speak, too." They have been married since before his first of seven attempts. Following the conference in Atlanta, they initiated the first statement on suicide to be adopted by the Episcopal Church, which was approved in the summer of 2000.

At present, OASSIS, with Ken and Madge, are looking toward a national conference for survivors of suicide attempts, their families, and friends. If that group is organized, whether or not they choose to call themselves "Children of Jonah," a major achievement in en-

---

4. Meri Nana-Ama Danquah, *Willow Weep for Me* (New York: Ballantine Books, 1999).

riching lives will have taken place. As the National Strategy for Suicide Prevention states, "Everyone who is touched by suicide has a contribution to make."

About These Stories

Those who here tell of their attempts, their thoughts and emotions at the time, and their later reflections are from different ages, races, locations, national origins, social levels, professions, and economic backgrounds. Most are or have been married; some not. They speak of different methods and circumstances.

Suicidologists maintain there is no single cause for a person's taking his or her own life. Yet each of these accounts reveals similar inner corridors of mind and soul—hellish despair, tormented dreams, anguished doubt, lashing rage, profound probing, forgiving spirits, continuing concerns—all are included, sometimes in the same account.

Not all choose to tell their story, and we must honor their decision with full respect. It has been said by some who have spoken or written, however, that for all the pain involved, it was a liberating experience.

To say the least, we need no longer assume that all such survivors wish to remain totally reclusive. Many might well wish to speak, and to be helped by doing so, if they knew others would listen with loving concern and understanding.

A number of figures in entertainment, sports, and media have recently made known their attempts. They have spoken of why they took the action, where and how they received treatment, what might have been done to prevent their attempt, what they have been doing since, and where they are now.

We are indebted to them for shedding light on an all-too-hidden issue and for helping to remove the stigma from themselves and others.

A Word on Terminology

One way of removing oppressive stigma is to stop referring to those who have taken their lives as having "committed suicide." The phrase only perpetuates a centuries-old belief that such people, regardless of their condition, motive, or circumstance, had committed a "crime" against the state or a "sin" against God.

For a while in England, the stigma was so bad that people who attempted and failed could be brought to trial and, if convicted, sentenced to death. It was a felony in many American states until recent years. Thanks to recent research, we know that most suicides are by people who suffer from one or more serious illnesses, often untreated, or by those who, once feeling good again, have gone off their medication. Although depression does not cause suicide, it is one of the two most common factors, the other being, as mentioned above, previous attempts. Bipolar and schizophrenic disorders and chemical deficiencies in the brain are other recognized factors.

Just as we never say a person "commits" brain tumor, stroke, or heart attack, so the decent, humane thing is to remove all traces of blame and shame. It is the considerate and just thing to do toward survivors and to the memory of their loved ones.

Likewise, "attempters" is not a word those who have survived a suicide attempt prefer. That in itself tends to stigmatize them as incompetents. More realistically, they are indeed "survivors" deserving of all the respect due any other person. Perhaps even a bit more.

—James T. Clemons, editor

1

A Letter from Iceland

Indíana Erna Þorsteinsdóttir

In December 2000 I was invited by a Lutheran pastor in Iceland to go there and assist him in offering pastoral care and suicide awareness to his parish after four suicides by young men there earlier that year. After my first meeting with their families, Indíana Erna told me of her companion's death and of her own attempt and struggles to get help in bringing survivors together.

—JTC

Dear Reader,

I'd like to start by telling you how I met James Clemons. Last year he attended an educational preventive suicide seminar here in Iceland. This little, but large, man captured my attention, and his fire and strength convinced me that this was a man worth listening to. In him I found someone who could help me.

Suicide! The meaning of suicide has held my mind and heart in captivity since the 11th of July 1999. That day my best friend, my fiancé, and the father of my unborn child took his own life. It is a day never to be forgotten. Here is my heart on a platter (my story).

He was 25 years old and his life hadn't been a bed of roses. He had fought a losing battle against drugs and alcohol since the age of twelve. There must be something broken, something that happens in the body or the mind of an individual who takes his own life, something that compels one to act out this crime. Is it a sickness, a personal weakness or pure psychosis? Nothing justifies or causes suicide. There is no crime as selfish, and I do mean crime against yourself and those who love and respect you.

Funny, given his problems, that describes my fiancé well. He was loved and respected not only by me, his family, and his friends, but by many others who knew him or had heard of him. He was a very talented musician and a role model to aspiring younger musicians. He was a drummer in a rock group when he died and had played with numerous bands in his career. Despite his young age, he had published cassettes and a CD. Ironically, his own music was played at his funeral.

As I said earlier, he battled with drugs and alcohol for a long time. He had gone through many rehabilitations without success. His dream was to have an ordinary drug-free life. There were drug-free periods, but they didn't last, and finally he made up his mind to try to help other addicts by sharing his life's story with them. He is the reason I'm drug-free today.

It was a beautiful, warm, sunny Tuesday and I was in high spirits on the way to my fiancé in the company of two close friends. Another friend had taken his life on the 28th of June which was a shock to me because he had been at the same level as I was only weeks earlier. Now, though still grieving and pregnant, I felt like my life had taken a turn for the better. Three months after I found out I was pregnant, I decided to take a big step and move back to my family. I felt I couldn't stay in the drug-filled environment my fiancé and I had lived in. I was determined to rid myself of the drug habit and went through the worst withdrawal symptoms on a camping trip with my parents while my sister competed in a swim meet in a town nearby.

The weekend before, we had spent together. We weren't living together but we were together. He was still in a world I didn't belong to anymore, a world I couldn't stay in, even visit, but we belonged together. He had had serious mood swings in that last month, before I moved away. Joy and depression linked with fits of tears. He wanted to make us a good home. He decorated our apartment with paintings and ornaments. He wanted to clean our slate financially. He became a regular Mr. Tidy. He washed the windows, floors, and walls as well as everything else. A guest would put out a cigarette and he'd jump and wash the ashtray. To me this was a bit extreme, but then he'd always been a very tidy person and I took this as preparation to make our unborn child a good home. That Saturday night he drove me home and we said our good-byes tenderly, very much in love.

I hadn't felt so good in a long time, but felt there was some uncertainty in my heart because he hadn't called. I went to his house with friends. When we reached his street a chilling fear ran down my spine—there was a police car outside his house and my first thought was that this had to be a drug bust. I left my friends in the car and walked to the house where I met three police officers. They were all wearing protective gloves and one was carrying a large briefcase. They asked where I thought I was going and, upon hearing, they asked what relations I had to him. I told them I was his fiancé and the next thing I knew one of them says, "He's dead, committed suicide!"

Time stopped, I felt like my heart had been ripped out and stomped on. The world swirled and I fell down, threw up, and fainted all in one motion. When I came to, I stood up and attempted to gather my senses. My limbs were numb and I had a hard time breathing. The policemen just stood there, probably without a clue of what to do or say.

My mind refused to register the information given. "This must be a lie! This cannot be true! Not him! Not the father of my unborn child! Not this life-loving person I knew!" I unloaded a barrage of questions on them. What did he do to himself? There was a long silence, as if they were weighing the problem at hand. Finally one of them decided to tell me.

"He hanged himself and we just finished cutting him down."

That was it. My heart stopped pounding and the tears finally came and I couldn't stop crying. As my heart cried, my thoughts took me back a few months. We had talked about how we would die, causes, and funerals. He had told me his worst nightmare was to die by hanging. Had there been a hidden agenda? This thought was an added shock.

The day after his death I went to our former apartment and found it in total shambles. Everything he had worked so hard to build and maintain had been destroyed. Furniture had been thrown around, everything was off the walls and broken into pieces. Six hours prior to the pronounced time of his death, I had been in his apartment and it had been perfect.

Now, this is what happens after the fact. Why? Why him? Why now? Why didn't I do this? Or that? If I would have . . . ? I should have been with him? If . . . then maybe he would still be alive? Self-doubt that eats at your sanity. Then I became angry. Angry with God. How could God allow this to happen? My anger stole my belief in a higher power. If there was a higher power, this wouldn't have been allowed to happen.

> *Why did you break*
> *my little heart?*
> *We always could shake*
> *the mean ugly past.*

Hey! You just left me with lies.
We're alone, just our baby and I.
Open your dead eyes,
You didn't just kill yourself!
Why!?

—INDÍANA ERNA

Then I started reading, reading books about the higher power, about the act of suicide and some self-help books. Among many, one book really stood out and helped me through my most desperate hours. *Conversations with God* is its name, and one sentence kept repeating itself in my mind: "God gave us the freedom to make our own choices as well as the Ten Commandments."[1] I cannot believe that God, our creator, can watch us, wants us to destroy ourselves.

Why
I just stood there and looked at you die.
Why the hell couldn't I do something? Why!
Now I have my beautiful baby boy.
Can you see?
Does he look like you or does he look like me?
He has beautiful blue eyes.
In them I see no lies.
My beautiful boy saved me.
Why can't all the people see?
Why didn't you let him save your soul?
He has no father, that was your role.
I looked into your eyes

1. Neale Donald Walsch, *Conversations with God*, vol. 1 (New York: Putnam's Sons, 1996).

and saw only lies.
Big, black eyes.
In them, I just saw death.
　　　　—INDÍANA ERNA

Isn't it unbelievable, that someone would rather die than ask those closest to them for help? Is that pride at its worst? From the outside looking in, there is nothing that cannot be amended or solved with those you love. But I've been on the other side of that wall too and I've felt alone in a world that was suffocating me: things like losing a loved one, being in financial ruin, uncontrollable drug addiction, an overwhelming feeling of guilt and shame.

I was only thirteen when I first attempted to take my life by cutting (severely scratching, actually) my wrists and taking a bunch of pills. Three months earlier I got drunk for the first time, at a girlfriend's house. I couldn't handle the liquor and passed out. When I came to I was being raped. My only prior sexual experience was innocent kissing. As it went, I did not report the rape to the police, but I felt I had brought this onto myself. This contributed to a feeling of guilt and shame that I couldn't overcome and I didn't think this would ever change. My mother found me and through limited consciousness I watched her bring me back. I will never forget the look on her face and the tears streaming down her face as she saved me.

The second attempt was in a storm on New Year's Eve 1997. That time I threw myself into the ocean (from a pier) after a period of depression brought on by drugs and a terrible lifestyle. My boyfriend at the time dragged me out of the freezing Atlantic and convinced me to stay.

The third one was a serious attempt to end my life as well as the life of my unborn as I was almost three months pregnant. I had been doped for three weeks straight not leaving the house, hardly sleeping or eating. I overdosed quite on purpose. I had never injected any-thing close to so much and I thought this would kill me for sure. My last thoughts were on the future, it would have nothing to do with me. I felt my family had deserted me and I didn't want to continue living this hell I had created. A life that only the devil could have thought up.

I'm in the unique position of understanding from what hell the fa-ther of my child thought he was escaping when he decided to end his life. I wish I could have told him there is another way. Today I have a beautiful son, my own apartment, a job, and I'm going to school as well. I am working with children, adults, the elderly, drug addicts, the disabled, and the sick. Every day I tell myself how lucky I am to be alive, to see and hear, to be able to express myself, and to be healthy. Each day is precious and no matter how badly it ends, another day will be born at sunrise, with new hopes and dreams waiting to be fulfilled.

Bright Flame (Bjartur Logi)

In memory of Kristinn Rúnar Ingason (born March 2, 1974; deceased July 11, 1999), my fiancé and the father of our child, Bjartur Logi.

Why didn't you see the beautiful light
Our baby in my belly, save you he might.
Now you lie in the ground
and I'm stuck here, alone all around.

—INDÍANA ERNA

Here are the poems of others who have suffered as I have.

Heaven, heaven take me to you
and tell me that I've been dreaming.
Heaven, heaven take me to you

take me to where I belong.
Heaven, heaven take me to you
and let me forget everything.

—ÁSLAUG PERLA
[WRITTEN IN 1999, ONLY MONTHS BEFORE
SHE WAS BRUTALLY MURDERED]

It's cold but the sun warms you
It gets dark but the moon lights your path
There are no clouds to restrain you
And your star follows you home.

—UNKNOWN

— — —

Today, Indíana Erna is raising her son in her home town. She works at a daycare center as well as for the local social services department, working with troubled teenagers. She continually educates herself on all things concerning self-help, coping with grief, and staying clean of drugs. Indíana Erna has spoken publicly of the world of drug use, in churches and schools, and with public officials. She is currently assisting suicide prevention groups to organize fund-raising concerts.

Dancing
with Death

DeQuincy A. Lezine

Quix Lezine has spoken on several occasions to suicide conferences across the country and was one of two African Americans on the OASSIS-sponsored Interfaith Conference on Religion and Suicide panel on Survivors of Attempted Suicide. While a student at Brown University, he founded the first campus chapter of the Suicide Prevention Advocacy Network. He is now a graduate student in psychology at UCLA.   —JTC

When I crossed the interstate, I'm not sure how intent I was on being hit by a sixteen-wheel truck. I was feeling so estranged from myself that nothing really mattered any more. I no longer felt the sense of identity that I had before I left high school. I'd had a definite social role before, and a definite place to fit in. Suddenly it was as if I'd looked up and that was all gone. Once that realization hit me, I no longer knew just who I was.

There was also this voice in my head daring me to cross, urging me to take that chance. Rather than auditory hallucination, it was more like the internalization of all the taunts and teasing I had endured in the years previous. It had become part of me, that criticizing, relentless, and angry voice continuing to torment me. Before that point I had always been able to exercise self-control and keep my behavior in check despite the hounding inner critic. The inhibitions were gone though, and there was no use in holding back because I didn't feel that was worth it. I crossed as if to say to that inner critic, "I'm no longer afraid of death." That is a scary thought when you think about it. I was just a step away from "I'm ready to die."

When I made it across, it was exhilarating because I felt almost freed from the "burden" of caution. It was the same feeling when I ran down the bus tunnel, a long stretch of tunnel that goes from the bottom of the hill to the top used only for public transportation. In some ways I was hoping for a bus to come because there would be no way out once I had committed to going into the tunnel. Part of me clearly wanted to die, and getting past that initial commitment was a step in that direction. In some ways I was hoping to make it through to the other side because I would have won the "game." Thus, I suppose, part of me also wanted to break free from the caution that had led to social derision before. I wanted to get out of the life I had before, and I was leaving the method to chance. I guess it was like the feeling gamblers get once they've made their bid—that anxious excitement gave me such a rush, and the stakes could not have been higher. It was the ultimate wager: life.

Shortly before I was committed to a psychiatric hospital, I was on top of a parking garage, eight stories up, with the wind beating my brow as I looked out over the city where I had my first dance with death. There was a hurricane warning so there weren't many people out and it was quite wet out in the open. I could see the section of interstate that I crossed, the bus tunnel, parts of the university, and areas of town where long night walks had found me at midnight. I had been to this spot before and backed down because I convinced myself that I had some purpose in life.

This time, though, it seemed like there was absolutely nothing to look forward to. My best friend was out of town, my high school friends were at other schools, my family was over 3,000 miles away, most of the campus was out on vacation, and I felt like I had a giant hole in my chest. I climbed up onto the concrete barrier, fully ready to meet the pavement below with open arms. Suddenly, a huge gust of wind hit me and knocked me into the housing of the stairwell I used to access the roof. Needless to say, it was both shocking and painful. I took it as a sign that some higher power really didn't want me to die that night.

Some agree, some say it was luck, others dismiss it as coincidental, and most doubt that the event ever happened at all. I was depressed, but not demented—it happened.

Not long after I got out of the psychiatric hospital, when my dad said that he didn't care whether or not I died, I didn't really know how to react. What thoughts were supposed to cross my mind when he talked about taking my ashes "back home" to Louisiana to let them be carried off with the wind? He talked to me for over two and a half hours, a tirade of sorts meant to make him feel better, but meanwhile it ripped me apart.

I walked out of the house and on to the street. I walked down the street, keeping to my side of the road while cars rolled by the other side bearing drivers with looks mixed with fear and wonder. I stopped once I got to the middle of a major intersection, and there, on the double yellow lines, I sat down. Solemnly I watched the headlights approach and wondered how many drunk drivers were on the street that New Year's Eve at about 11 p.m. Some honked, some yelled, some shouted unintelligibly as their automobiles rushed by. Eventually though, as I was depressed, I even became habituated to that dangerous situation. I felt the rush of air as cars passed at about 45 m.p.h. not more than a foot away from where I sat. I saw the glare of five to ten sets of headlights daring me to move as they sped downhill towards my location. Unscathed and in many ways disappointed by the lack of lawless driving, I made my way home via the middle of the street.

I can't say that the same level of excitement was present when I was walking the train tracks, though. Deep in sorrow and confused about my romantic life (or lack thereof), I was very honestly wishing for a train to come. When one didn't come barreling down the tracks to end my miserable existence, I felt disappointed. My heart sank when I realized that I had to keep living, as if living was a curse. I fell to my knees and begged for God to strike me down with lightning, have the earth swallow me, or in some other way end my life. That was a suicidal gamble with different intentions.

Since all of those situations happened within my first year at college, it was evidently a problem, but my intent was questioned. Some say that I was feeling disconnected from my family, but I left Los Angeles to be apart from them. Some say that I was too stressed with the new academic demands, but I was getting A's in all of my classes. Some say I was just trying to get attention, but I walked off alone and made sure that nobody saw me leave. Some, however, would watch as teardrops slowly burned down my face in lonely shadows that night and say that I was depressed. Not depressed like the everyday blues, or "something just went wrong," or best-friend-moved-away, or a pet dies, but clinically depressed. So utterly dejected that when I climbed the fence of the interstate, I had no concern for my safety or even my life. When I trotted across the interstate, I made it clear that I was so depressed that death became an option. You might still question whether any of those events qualify as suicide attempts; after all, many professionals do.

"If you really want to die," so the myth goes, "you try to shoot yourself or hang yourself or cut yourself or something." Could I really have been that intent on dying since I didn't act in one of the ways traditionally identified as suicide attempts? Is taking a gamble with your life serious enough to be called a suicide attempt? There are several ways to answer this question.

First, taking a gamble with your life indicates a low value placed on something that is considered precious by most standards. Most people fight for the right to have better health care, medical insurance, and safety regulations because we generally want to live as long as possible. I could only leave death to chance once I felt that my own life wasn't worth fighting for. Isn't that a red flag indicating that something is gravely wrong?

Second, when I took those gambles, I felt like there wasn't much to care about, let alone planning a method of self-destruction. I had no particular desire to expend the energy working out a "traditional" suicide attempt, but because I also didn't care about my life, I placed myself in those positions. Such lack of feeling is a rather common theme for many who have suffered severe depression and seems indicative of the same numbness that could later result in suicide.

In addition, I viewed these as preliminary stages preparing my mind and body for self-inflicted death. Suicide is not something that is accomplished without effort, driven by both serious intentions and psychological pain. Living is such a basic biological drive that it is extremely difficult to overcome that basic instinct to continue. For me, leaving life or death to chance was only the beginning of something I fully intended to complete.

Two noted scholars in the field of suicide, Beck and Greenberg, wrote that those who gamble with death are uncertain about dying but serious enough "to take a definite risk with their own lives."[1] Thus, they equated these individuals with others of serious intent. Furthermore, I think it is extremely dangerous to fail to recognize

1. Aaron T. Beck and Ruth Greenberg, "The Nosology of Suicidal Phenomena: Past and Future Perspectives," *Bulletin of Suicidology* (American Association of Suicidology, 1995).

this type of attempting as serious suicidal behavior. When someone asks, "What did you do?" they're expecting something from the traditional list of attempts. They want to hear about cutting or jumping or hanging or drowning or shooting. It's almost like if you didn't do one of the things on that limited list, then whatever you did just doesn't count as a suicide attempt, at least to the health care professionals and the media. I know that in my case such responses were partial motivations for my later self-cutting and overdose attempts. It is probably true for others as well, and if that holds for attempted suicide, then regrettably it can be applied to some suicide deaths as well.

On the other hand, my friends were all extremely concerned about me, fully realizing that it was not a large step from gambling with death to seriously courting it. However, they also had information about how I acted prior to my attempts. I was known for being virtually stress-free and relaxed in the face of pressure or hard demands. I had been extremely cautious about taking risks and conservative about putting myself in the way of danger. Going from a reserved person to one leaving life or death to chance outcomes was a huge leap that indicated a very dangerous trend. It was only a matter of time before my flirtations with death became perilously close to being irreversible.

One question that logically follows is, "What was going on in your mind when you were doing all this?" or "How did you feel?" Most of my feelings were recorded in e-mail messages and poetry. When deeply depressed, I found poetry to be an expressive outlet that came naturally. Hence, my poetry was the window to the darkness within.

The Man Confused
Why? Why! Why.
Why me? Why now?
Do I laugh? Do I cry?

Do I stand? Do I bow?
Do I love? Do I feel?
Do I care? Should I show?
Do I rise? Do I kneel?
Do I know? I don't know.

Why is she doing this to me?
Why doesn't she know what I do?
Why can't she see—doesn't see—
What is it that I can't give to you?
What is it I'm afraid to be?
What can't I give without revealing
within this man a child who's kneeling?
What path is it that I'm afraid to go
because what lies ahead I don't know?

Why. Why! Why?
Why does she care so much?
Doesn't she know it's only I?
How does a man say he's touched?
I say "I care" I don't feel like a man—
I say "I love you" and I'm not full grown—
but I'm not made of stone and
why? must I? I've never known.

Confusion was one of the foremost feelings for me because I found myself in positions that were unfamiliar to me. The most confusing was dealing with interpersonal feelings, most notably affection. The first stanza of the previous poem is a man asking himself what to do once he's found out that someone is interested in him. I had no idea how to respond when I discovered that a friend of mine was romantically attracted to me. I could not identify my own emotions and, what's more, I was afraid to feel what I had kept myself from feeling for so long. In addition, those around me were giving me conflicting bits of advice. The situation was so intensely frustrating that I would have preferred death to trying to work through it.

That, however, was only one of the many confusing aspects of my life at that time. I didn't know what my place was in my family anymore since I had moved out and was living on the opposite coast. I had not found a social niche at college and thus wondered what place I was supposed to have on campus. I knew a large number of people but was unsure of who my real friends were.

Another point of extreme confusion was what my future was going to be like. I had put so much effort into dreaming about going off to college and out of the city I used to live in that I had not planned beyond that. I aspired to get to college and worked hard to make that happen, but once that goal was attained, I was left without any real goals. What was I supposed to do now? Truthfully, I had no idea.

On the Edge

Where is The Edge? Let me tell you about
the place I walk now, what lures me
there at night, and now I can't get out
let me show you what I see . . .
when I close my eyes,
when I shut my mind to the outside
when I wish I could fly
out over the expanse of pain I hide.

It is peaceful, it is quiet, it is still
like the air beneath me as I fall.
I lived for as long as I held that will

but on the other side I give up all.
On one side of this razor line I walk
is a world called euphoria, the release
on the other side, I really want to talk
but my pain demands a release.

All of the feelings, all of the sorrow
I've got tied up and chained in my heart
makes me wonder if there will be tomorrow
or if this pain will finally tear me apart.
I felt so good the other day, if only I could stay
as happy as I was, but so often I have found
that nothing good can ever stay that way
so I'm back at the top, staring down at the ground.

It's messing up my head.
I'm wishing I was dead.
I wanted love, I did,
but I got pain instead.
I tried to get ahead,
but my pain you've fed . . .
Maybe I'd be better dead . . .
Perhaps if I step off the ledge
the other side of the hedge
—the grass is greener on that side—
—no more fears or pain to hide—
—I'm still living on the outside—
—how long I've been dead inside—
Forgive me for stepping from the ledge
I'm not living anymore on the edge . . .
I'm not living anymore . . .
I'm not living . . .

I'm not giving . . .
I'm not deceiving . . .
I'm not breathing . . .
I'm not . . . anymore.

If you had asked me whether or not I wanted to die I would have told you very honestly that I didn't know, but also that I was leaning towards death. I feel the previous poem expresses that point quite well, along with the avenues through which I was trying to decide. Split by an edge as sharp as a razor blade, there were two decisions as different as night and day: to live or not to live. I felt like I was walking along that edge and swaying back and forth between which decision to choose. All I knew for certain is what I said in the first stanza, I wanted to get away from the immense pain that I felt. I think that's a theme that's common for many who have suicidal thoughts.

The second verse describes the dilemma that I was facing, the one that made me so indecisive. On the one hand I wanted to talk out my troubles, get everything resolved, and continue living. On the other hand, the pain was so great that the urge to end it was unbearable enough to push me toward death. The certainty of having no more pain was a very enticing option when it seemed near certain that, if I continued to live, there would only be more pain to add to what I was already suffering. This debate continued into the third verse by expressing that I realized that there would be good days; after all, I had experienced some. However, most of those good times were brought to an end, which made me question whether such joy was merely illusory. I had no desire to live if that would only entail chasing after elusive dreams and ending up in terrible pain each time. The poem then ends by citing that I searched for love and got pain, I looked for success and received the same, and thus I began questioning the value of death as an alternative.

In the language of decisions and logic, death is an option, despite what many would like to argue. If it wasn't an option then nobody could take it, and, as the statistics show, over 30,000 people a year choose to die. I think it's more important to start asking why some people decide on that option rather than arguing about the validity of calling it an option. If it is a possible outcome that is decided upon (consciously or unconsciously), then it is an option. It is that simple. Usually we don't think of it as an option because we can see so many more desirable alternatives that it doesn't even enter our minds as something viable. As I outlined in my poem, however, when subjective alternatives are limited because of depression, and even those are further limited because of circumstances, then death not only becomes a viable option, it becomes a very attractive one. As my options were eliminated, the probability of choosing one of the remaining alternatives continued to rise. To miss that fact is to ignore potential danger.

He looked at me with those happy eyes
he has and he cracked a crooked smile
than other types he like I
and only He had carefully counted the miles
I've walked where when none knew—
Pacing out the distance of darkness—
He looked at me and that Brown rang true:
of manhood held pride tested and met.

Would you really like to take a peek inside
the cavernous realm of haunts and nightmares?
It's a warning, this, there's no place to hide
'cause walls torn down not rebuilt in there
where shadows live to speak stalk shout yell!!

Gloom is good. Up is down. Blue is gold.
Home is real; love exists; tis' not hell
and reality marries Stories I've told.

I see it, our eyes speak my lingo kid
so it's no use denying worry nature called.
I was once worried, till to this state slid
whence now before me dreams mine fall,
suicidal death awaits the last morsels of earth
taken from blue strips of a Band-Aid
we nicknamed Society yet it holds so lil' worth
to "civilized" welfare none could save.

Yea, mark please my tombstone when journey is done,
"Transaction denied. Insufficient funds."

They call out though, pangs of sympathy cries
keeping me living through tumultuous days
wondering who chooses who lives or dies
and at times wishing cop plea to maybe say
"Allow me Cross, that line, into Otherman's land"
and NO! Now they shall look for me to "Be safe."
They will want to "talk" and won't really understand
this near-transcendental type mind-state.

My spirit afflicted, My mind is so ill . . .
They might come to look to find to capture me
to again lock me in chambers unreal
to dehumanize to scrutinize to analyze me
but NO! Time changes all but change itself.
The 8th story. The Year it binds. I they shall not see
at lab, at work, at room, at their twisted Brand X help
NO! But cement-indented-fatal may they find me.

Oh, but I suffer still a madness destructive
that traps not body but the mindspace and takes
a man's instinct of survival, the very will to live
the temporal management, the biological rape
genetically timed to so ravage itself and no
Oh God! I am asking a wondering of my mind's weather:
Tis' storm-typhoon windswept with thunder; Allow,
if you will, one lonely young troubled son to get better?

In mania and in mixed states of mania and depression, there was a sense of chaos in the mind that sent thoughts of death racing along the twisted synaptic highways of my brain. The second stanza documents how I perceived what was going on as a collage of deceit, fantasy, and negative experiences. The result was comparable to the ruins of a city after a drawn-out war, with my mind ravaged and shaken to the foundations. The third stanza states what I mentioned earlier, that I was no longer afraid of death or worried about what would happen because I was expecting the worst.

When I wrote that "they call out" I was referring to the friends whose rationalizations kept me alive even when I saw no reason for living. Every one of the hundred or so thoughts that went through my mind each minute pointed to death, so I was practically begging to be allowed to die. Under the constant barrage of suicide-centered thoughts, my will to live was worn down and the biological urge to continue was withering. It seemed to be only a matter of time before all that held me from falling over the edge atrophied.

Reconstruction

Under Reconstruction—
This site will soon be

a marvelous construction,
a brand new me.

Some stones I'm sure you'll recognize,
broken glass made mosaic by art,
some things here might surprise
but here and there are old parts—

'cause though the old's demolished . . .
Some things need to be remade today
or cleaned and renovated and polished
and some—crushed and swept away.

Under New Supervision—
Come and try, you'll see
the effects of my decision
to craft a brand new me.

Not all of the thoughts were aimed at self-destruction as you can see, although the majority were. There were times when I felt like I had been through a rough time but would be able to take that experience, learn from it, and make myself better. I knew that some of what I believed before was unreasonable and that many of my expectations (of self and others) were grandiose. I sometimes saw it as possible to take the good parts from my past, discard the ones that took me towards suicide, and work on improving the rest. Those were brief and sporadic times, but somewhere in the back of my mind the will to live was a very strong force. It was much like internal warfare, fighting for life or death. Unfortunately, the more things beyond my subjective control went wrong, the stronger the side edging towards death became.

Lost World

What has it all come to? How things do change . . .
What once I believed I found untrue
and once I thought life well arranged
and once I had faith in what I knew.
Like a fairy tale with "Once upon a time"
beginning the illustrious work of fiction
crafted by idealists; the dreamers sublime
tale of how it should be, in poetic diction.
So too, my life has turned out to be
one grand illusion to all it seems
until time and circumstance awakened me
to the reality obscured by the dreams.

Thought I had control once, I did
but by events I was controlled
except emotions devastatingly hid
deep within the dark of my soul.
Thought I was smart, I can still recall
thinking I knew so very much,
but I, the fool, was played by all
and I, blindly stayed out of touch.
Thought I great, came I insane.
Thought I strong, came I to fall.
Thought I unique, found I the same.
Thought I grand, found I small.
My world been upside-down turned
as I see my released pain and scars
facing how so long I've been burned
fighting valiantly a nonexistent war.

Like Don Quixote have I fought windmills
to save the honor of the dishonorable one
and seeing the giant did I thus kill,
dreaming the impossible dream—the son
of a working man . . . the ambitious hero
and was it, after all has been brought out
worth ending each time with a zero?
Or is that what my life's about?
Nothing is quite the same anymore I'll say . . .
My world of fantasy or illusion or dream
shattered, flipped, turned, shifted into mess.

At one point in time I believed that I was the master of my own fate, but once I became depressed and began retrospectively analyzing my life, I saw things differently. It seemed like I never really had control over anything in my life and that everything I did was merely reactionary. My emotions and behaviors didn't seem of my own volition, and thus I felt hopeless about altering my current situation. It was like some other force had doomed me to a life of suffering. Throughout the poem I was saying that I had such great dreams, and in reality they were impossible. To come to such a conclusion was incredibly self-defeating and it crushed the little self-esteem I had.

Moreover, having a shift in my perceived locus of control (or how much of my life I had control over) had profound effects on my thoughts about death. Why couldn't I immediately control my own death? Hence, it seemed fitting that since fate had chosen my life of suffering, it should also kill me. When I attempted to end my life in the ways described previously, it was I placing myself in a position where an external factor would result in my death. Perhaps if I had been led to conceive of myself as having more control over the negative events in my life, I would have been more prone to choose one of the forms of attempting that involves more self-directed means of harm.

So now you might ask, what factors led to my perception of an external-locus-of-control and gambling type of suicide attempt?

There has been considerable discussion about the possibility of genetic factors that predispose someone to mental illness and thus suicidal behavior. These range from inherited differences in temperament to levels of neurotransmitters (or the chemical messengers in the brain). As a result, it is customary for a psychiatrist seeing a new patient to inquire about family history of mental illness. Because of the taboo surrounding mental illness, actual diagnoses don't come up in conversation very often. However, some things can be pieced together. Alcoholism was rampant on both sides of my family practically as far back as anyone could remember. There was also drug abuse on both sides of the family. There is definitely evidence pointing to the likelihood of genetic factors in my family tree.

On my mom's side of the family are alcoholism, drug abuse, attention-deficit hyperactivity disorder (ADHD), and depression at the least. My mom has been addicted to alcohol, cocaine, and other narcotics. My aunt had some problems with alcohol and was on medication for clinical depression. Their brother also had bouts of depression that he was on medication for. Both my mom and aunt had attempted suicide in the past. My maternal grandmother and grandfather both died of cancer, and they were heavy drinkers as well. Drug abuse was common among my cousins, who also tended to be depressed, and my only first cousin on the maternal side was diagnosed with ADHD (although there was some severe conduct disorder as well).

On my dad's side of the family are alcoholism, drug abuse, mania, depression, and psychotic symptoms. My father drinks heavily and is most likely manic-depressive, although he's never been officially diagnosed. At least two of my paternal aunts and one uncle were on medication for psychotic symptoms. At least one paternal aunt was being treated for depression. One uncle had been diagnosed as manic-depressive. Both paternal grandparents drank heavily and were chain smokers. My brother also suffers from bouts of depression and extremes in mood, and was diagnosed with OCD (obsessive-compulsive disorder) at one point. It is no wonder that my genetic history is considered "loaded," as one psychiatrist put it.

According to the diathesis-stress model that is the leading model for modern psychiatry, in addition to predisposing biological factors there are usually environmental factors to trigger the mental illness. I grew up in a rather strict family environment where corporal punishment was most often used as discipline. Whether the threats were real or imagined, I learned to keep my thoughts to myself and ignore my feelings because expressing them often only got me in trouble. It's been stated that children of alcoholics learn three fundamental rules: Don't talk. Don't feel. Don't think. I had the first two down within a short amount of time, but the last was more problematic. I couldn't just deny what was going on around me and I was very self-aware, so instead of learning not to think, I became depressed as a child.

The threat of divorce was something I remember feeling almost two years before the event actually happened (when I was about eight years old). Not surprisingly, that was the first time I thought about committing suicide. It was very late at night, probably about midnight, and both my father and brother were asleep. My mom had gone out roller skating and I was still up because I was waiting for her to come home. I was very worried about her safety, and the thoughts entering my head were of car trouble, accidents, or attackers. I had the sinking feeling that things weren't going to turn out well. Staring into the dark kitchen, I fell asleep contemplating the possibility of death using a knife from the top drawer. I was not a happy kid.

The surroundings were not much brighter in that part of Los Angeles with its drug dealers, murders, gangs, imposing police presence, crime, and poverty. I can never forget seeing a next-door neighbor carried out on a stretcher with his head busted open over something to do with drugs. I didn't get to spend much time with my cousins because most of them were in gangs or serving time behind bars. One of my cousins shot a man in the back as part of a gang initiation, and he ended up spending most of his time in jail or with the gang. Hearing about a huge fight between a paternal aunt and uncle, which involved a hatchet and resulted in jail time along with a broken arm, will be seared into my mind forever. At school there were bullies, thugs, kids with guns, kids with knives, and security guards with vendettas, as well as administrators concerned with corporate politics. The teachers went on strike because they weren't being paid enough, and the good teachers spent from their limited personal budgets to get us supplies. No matter what people aspired to or talked about achieving or dreamed about getting, it seemed like everyone ended back in the streets eventually.

With all that as a backdrop, there was a tremendous need for some academic hero, or gifted black kid, or school leader that I thought could fill those shoes. They were large shoes to fill because they would be taken as representative to the community, African Americans, youth, my family, and so much more. In a way I was expected to and came to expect myself to make up for everything else that was happening by doing nothing short of perfection. I had to get straight A's and play sports and be involved in the community and tutor and speak on behalf of others and not let anything get me down. Those impossible roles, some stated overtly and some stated amidst a myriad of subtleties, were internalized and shaped into something I believed I was. Of course, it helped that I had a straight-A average in high school, was part of the community, tutored others, was a leader when it was expected, and made my family proud. In a way, though, all of that made me even more vulnerable to feeling inadequate later. With perfection as not only an ideal but also an expectation for myself, once anything went wrong, the entire facade would crumble, leaving me feeling like a worthless failure. In part that's what happened once my depression surfaced during my first semester at college.

Return to the Edge

Why should I keep living this life I've got
when nothing in life is guaranteed
except for the jump into the empty lot
whereupon from this pain I'd be freed?
I hate having to continue with such hurt
when my life spins without meaning
and my being twists without worth,
so come one, come all, first screening
of the end of the Quix, the last call
to see what happens to a man destroyed,
to a star that has seen his own fall,
to one scarred since he was a boy.

I laugh at what you would call living,
because I never had what you thought
I had, I was always used to giving
the illusion of joy that everyone bought

since I performed my part so well
that each was fooled by their own delusion
that I walked on clouds, when I was in hell
and they shocked at the sudden conclusion
to a life that people envied so often
to someone they styled a role model,
but I hoped that this blow I could soften
and that in my treads none would follow.

I gamble with my soul, I toss it to chance
and roll with what the dice might decide.
In the middle of the street my song and dance
in defiance of friends who had lied
when they promised truth, swore care,
and said that they would be here for me . . .
'cause when I looked, none were there
and I determined I'd be alone indefinitely.

Why, I ask, would none consider this one,
more afraid than friend, though as friend I was always
loyal and true, serious and yet fun,
faithful, helpful, and supportive each day?
Even I, as hard as I might try each time,
am abandoned by every friend I ever had
and alone again I'm sure to find
myself as things again go from good to bad.

Like a spiral, a downward twisting tunnel
of death that continues to drag me down,
all that could happen is funneled
into having me staring down at the ground

and standing here once more I fear,
wondering which side of the ledge
I should take, though the one looks most clear . . .
so here I stand, again . . . at The Edge.

Once everything had crumbled, I found myself on the edge quite literally, and thinking about making one final suicide attempt. I felt like "a star that has seen his own fall" because I had been built up so high (by myself and others) that becoming deathly depressed was comparable to being demolished. People kept telling me that I had so much to live for because of who I had been and what I had accomplished. They thought of that as indicative of what I had yet to achieve, but I saw it as evidence that I had lost everything that I once was. I had been fooling myself to believe that I was so untouchable, and others were deceived, too, because they wanted to believe that I was. We wanted to believe that so much that I ignored the pains, the bad memories, the suffering that I was holding inside. I stuffed away all the rage, discontent, loneliness, despair, hopelessness, fear, and doubt. They had considered me a role model and I didn't want to sully that image. I had no desire to stop them from believing that I could do the impossible because I wanted to believe it too. Once it seemed like all of that was ending, I felt like I not only had to face up to myself, but also to all those who looked up to me because I saw myself as letting them down. It was the most intense feeling of failure that I could ever imagine.

To the Funny Farm With Ye'

They came in blue and told me, "You've got to go with us."
Finished my electronic sentence, heart fell to floor,
hung head, tired walk . . . made my way no fuss . . .

As they "escorted" me through the glass doors
that held me within my electronic glory and pain,
put me in a squad car, carted Quix off to talk
about how nothing would ever again be quite the same
and buildings, and plans, and jumps, and long walks.
Accused of lacking love, of wanting to injure loved.
Accursed wretch knew nothing of my case . . . she assumed
and I asked "Why couldn't I die?" to my God above.
I still had much to live for I would presume.

Suggested I go to a "Hospital," not injured yet thought I.
Isn't that what you might need if you did not succeed
in your final bid to friends for end, to allow you to fly?
They said it was for my mind. For my mind? My heart
    did bleed
last drop of blood within, gave in, felt lost, felt bad . . .
I had lost it, the Quix held a mind no more
and my friends couldn't understand what had me so sad
or what had my heart down mopping the floor.
Now they threatened me with dismissal from my beloved
    school.
They said they couldn't let me do others that much
    harm, alarm
them and they explained all of their damned rules.
So I said "Fine, fuck it, take me away. Take me—to the
    Funny Farm."

I wanted to bid my friends farewell before I jumped off the building I had determined to be the highest point I could reach without
running into resistance. I had checked out the security, the accessibility of the stairwell and of reaching the point, and knew the time

when the fewest people would be passing the section of sidewalk below. My suicide note had been written on specialty paper that resembled green marble, stained with the rare tears I cried that night. I had written several e-mails to friends and I guess they made some calls because Police and Security came to pick me up from the computer cluster. I couldn't help but feel the last parts of my heart fall to the floor once that had happened and I was headed to the psychiatric hospital. I was signed in as "voluntary" but it was coerced by the Dean of Student Life. The day they checked me in to the hospital was the absolute lowest day of my life.

So, you might wonder, what happens after the attempts and hospitalization and I started on psychiatric mediation? In the hospital they gave me the diagnosis of depression after an interview skewed toward obtaining such a diagnosis that failed to follow the recommended guidelines. They put me on an antidepressant medication, although in truth I'm bipolar and doing so could have resulted in mania, which may have perpetuated another suicide attempt. The hospital stay was filled with activities and discussions that were extremely patronizing. We made snowflakes out of paper and talked about basic coping skills that seemed like common sense to me. Eventually I got bored. Although the hospital was one of the best, I can only think of that experience as dehumanizing and demoralizing.

After getting out of the hospital, I was faced with the intense stigma that accompanies suicide attempts and the mentally ill. On the one hand, since I survived my attempts, mental health professionals viewed my case as less serious. On the other hand, since attempting suicide is foreign to most people, many of my friends determined that it was too much for them to handle. The memory of one of my best friend's parents telling me to leave the family alone will be one that stays with me forever. He told me, "Nobody wants to be around a depressed person." He said that I was depressing to his daughter and that I shouldn't talk to her anymore. She felt the same way. Before all of this happened, however, her parents could not have been more encouraging towards our friendship since I was helping her develop into a more stable and confident person. For some people, everything changes once suicide enters the picture.

My parents and family no longer thought of me as being the capable person I was before attempting suicide, as if I had lost the capacity to function as a result. Suddenly I was supposed to "take it easy . . . don't push yourself . . . and make sure to ask for help if you need it." Hearing such loss of faith from even family was infuriating. My mom and dad started calling more often and being more worried about me. Previously I was the one to be concerned about others, but the tables had turned and now I was the one who "needed help." Nobody really understood what was going on inside of me, but everyone had their own solutions for my "problems." I was so fed up that I became more and more isolated from my family.

The insurance companies added to what was clearly an uphill battle by supplying me with red tape, bureaucracy, and piles of forms to fill out. Once I had to walk a mile and a half each way to a pharmacy on four separate occasions to obtain my prescribed medication because of computer problems at the insurance company. Each psychiatrist I saw had to be preauthorized, and forms had to be sent back and forth before I could get the medical attention I needed. Sometimes they refused to pay for medical treatment including blood tests, leaving me with hundreds of dollars of unpaid medical bills. It seems like instead of making the process of getting medical attention easier, they only added to the stress and frustration that exacerbated the original problem. Being denied medication because of some mix-up at the insurance company was enough to send me home thinking about jumping off a building again.

In the midst of all the turmoil that resulted from attempting suicide was the daunting task of trying to rebuild myself. From the start I knew that trying to put the pieces of my life back together was going to be a struggle. At times it was depressing just thinking about how much of myself seemed lost in the battle. I wrote friends telling them that I couldn't just "go back" to who I was before. That person seemed like either history or fiction to me.

I am NOT me.

He was a hero; I am no hero.
He was a role model; I am no role model.
Quix was 100% and I am zero.
I can be no leader for none would follow
a crazed, demented, neurotic nut case
now would they honestly? No . . .
Who do you see, it's not me behind this face . . .
Who is it? I really don't know.

He was great; I am not great.
He was ambitious; I don't ambition own.
Quix had friends but I can't relate
because sooner or later I'll stand alone . . .
He had dreams; mine are gone.
He had hope; I can't find it, 'tis lost.
I'm alive. Yes, my life shall go on
but my discoveries have had their cost.

Who am I now? Who's left for me to be?
The only roles I knew, rigidly fixed for so long
may not, I'll admit, truly have been me
but I swallowed my pain at least I looked strong.

I am hurting and everyone sees my pain.
I am helpless and everyone wants to help.
If not insane then perhaps they think I am inane?
Did they think it in vain that I chose myself
a name, worked for my fame, and lived to namesake?
Quixotic, neurotic, lunatic in a far-off city.
No more the hero, no more the leader, now the fake.
No more dignity, no more honor, only pity.
Somewhere, 'tween here and there, I lost me.

That poem addresses how I felt initially, but to continue living I knew that changes had to be made. Fortunately I considered change an ally instead of an enemy and had long prided myself on my ability to adapt. That was one ability that I did not feel I had lost.

My concentration could not be directed as easily as it was before. In mania my thoughts flew from topic to topic, and during depression I couldn't keep my mind on much more than suicide. I found something intensely motivating could keep my attention during hypomania, and the rapid thought process could even be channeled into making a convincing argument. With continued lithium usage, the number of fully manic episodes was kept to a minimum, so the combination of medication and finding more motivating subjects was effective.

During depression my thoughts were slowed to a near standstill and I often felt too drowsy to even begin my work. Again, nevertheless, a combination of antidepressant medications and more stimulating material was useful in continuing my studies. I also found that revising my expectations for work to get accomplished while depressed helped to keep my goals realistic and prevent me from becoming too disappointed. Since I was able to work, I started feeling worthwhile again and, thus, less suicidal or pessimistic.

Having lost my ability to perform the more mathematical-based tasks as a result of concentration deficits, my passion for creating through computer science was crushed. As if compensating for this, I found myself more drawn to psychology and mental health. I saw an incredible need for someone to be outspoken about suicide and mental illness, and I needed a role to fulfill that would benefit others. In many ways, it was a perfect fit. Treatment of mental illness and suicide prevention became the cause that fueled my academic and extracurricular efforts. Having lost most of my other roles, finding this new one was integral to the restructuring of myself that was taking place.

The risks that I took in the field of mental health advocacy and suicide prevention paid off with recognition and gratitude. The more I was called upon to speak about related issues, the more my self-esteem was rebuilt to a point where I felt I had a reason to continue living. It's been said so often that what someone needs is a personal reason to continue, and in many ways I had found my own personal reason. Increased self-esteem and confidence serve as safeguards against the feelings of hopelessness, helplessness, and negativity that foster suicidal feelings. For me, working to prevent the suicides and mental suffering of others helped to do the same for me.

I can't paint a rosy-colored picture of my life or give a "happily ever after" type of conclusion because I don't believe it is possible for me to be "fully recovered" from my dances with death. Suicide and suicidal feelings have been constantly with me since the first night I attempted, and I don't see them vanishing in spite of medication and therapy. There is still incredible stigma to face and insurance discrimination. There are still nights that I sit in the dark with a blade at my wrist and ask why I shouldn't kill myself. There are still times when I look at the building I had set for my final jump and imagine the freedom from all the psychological pain I suffer that could be had in death. Hardly a day goes by without the thought of suicide passing through my mind, no matter how happy or joyous the events around me are. Neither am I saying that I've given up or decided that since suicide can't be stripped from my life I should go through with it. On the contrary, I am saying that it is a worthwhile fight, but I refuse to grant the illusion that the struggle is not a continuing one.

A Moth
in the Heart

Paul Asbury Seaman

*Paul Seaman was an associate with the Churches Center for
Theology and Public Policy in Washington when we first met.
Soon after, I learned he had written a book on his experiences
as a boy growing up in Pakistan and that he was a survivor.[1]
Paul is married and lives in Gaithersburg, Maryland, with his
wife Rosalie.   —JTC*

When I was in high school, my favorite uncle killed himself. Uncle Joe was the pastor of a small United Methodist church in central Pennsylvania, just up the river from Three Mile Island. His thirteen-year-old son found him hanging from a pipe in the basement. Though he had struggled with emotional problems for many years, recently he seemed to have benefited from therapy and the positive results of marriage counseling were apparent in his family life. But some dark cloud of depression enveloped him anyway—literally choked him. A passing shadow, darker than the ocean's depths. It only took a moment.

1. Paul Asbury Seaman, *Paper Airplanes in the Himalayas: The Unfinished Path Home*, The West and Wider Series, vol. 13 (South Bend, Ind.: Cross Cultural Publications, 1997).

At the funeral, the presiding bishop read the following poem by Charles Hanson Towne, titled "Of One Self-Slain."

When he went blundering back to God,
His songs half written, his work half done,
Who knows what paths his bruised feet trod,
What hills of peace or pain he won?

I hope God smiled and took his hand,
And said, "Poor truant, passionate fool!
Life's book is hard to understand:
Why couldst thou not remain at school?"

The night before the funeral, the family had gathered in an alcove at the funeral home for a private wake. I remember the linoleum floor and the rows of folding chairs, an austerity that reflected the Appalachian context as much as the somber occasion. We were a big family—Dad had nine living brothers and sisters—and, with no one skilled in grief counseling or assertive enough to try, the whole big group of us sat in oppressive silence. Finally, one of my aunts suggested we pull our chairs around in a circle and talk about what we were feeling. So everyone got up and rearranged the folding chairs with a great clatter, more, I suspect, from relief at having something to do than from enthusiasm for the suggestion.

Then we sat in uncomfortable silence again, this time having to work harder at avoiding each other's eyes.

"I'll say something," I blurted out, my chest pounding. I stood up, blinking back tears. "I'm really angry at Uncle Joe. I think what he did was a fucking selfish thing to do. He abandoned his family and hurt a lot of people who loved him."

Well, that didn't exactly prime the pump. I think Aunt Sandy and my cousins understood, or did later, the pain behind my outburst, but Dad never forgave me. He thought I was just trying to get attention.

People don't like to talk about suicide. Talk about it, maybe—with a morbid fascination. Suicide is of course a recurring theme in "gothic" rock. And many people may not realize that the catchy theme music to the hit TV series MASH comes from the movie version's ironic song, "Suicide Is Painless." But curiosity, even sympathy, is not empathy—a compassion born of similar experience, or at least a focused effort to really understand.

Twenty years after Uncle Joe's funeral, I came very close to killing myself. I wasn't trying to get attention. I was just tired of life's struggles. I'm much happier now—most of the time. In spite of my own experience, I get impatient with people when they're really depressed. I don't know what to do. Even with my wife: I mean, what do you have to be depressed about? You've got a good life! You've got four wonderful kids who are all healthy; a good marriage; a good job. What's the matter with you? Quit being so self-indulgent. I don't say these things, but this is how I feel.

Yet, I too struggle with depression, with "self-indulgent" malaise —far more than my wife does. There have been at least three periods in my life when I felt suicidal. The first was in ninth grade, at a time when, ironically, I was very assertively trying to find a meaningful place in this life. The last time, when I was 35 years old, was the most serious. My recovery from that inclination is a story of initiative, hope, self-awareness, forgiveness, and the power of community. And, too, something beyond all these things that simply leaves me silent in awe at the mystery of it. But there remains another story of incomplete redemption, and that is why this book is important.

The last several years have been a time of catharsis, healing, and conscious growth. Yet, depression in its various and often subtle forms continues to limit me. It holds me back from opportunities that would stabilize my situation and enhance my self-esteem; it undercuts my effort to pursue even the things I love to do; it keeps me from experiencing life to the fullest. Occasionally, for fleeting moments, after a bad argument with my wife or some other incident that fills me with a sense of failure or uselessness, suicide still seems like an option. Of course, this is crazy—my marriage, with its reliable companionship, sense of belonging, and reassuring feedback, contributes greatly to my reasons for wanting to be alive.

But the inclination toward suicide is like an addiction. Like alcoholism, it is a temptation from which some of us are never fully cured. We learn to cope. As with any debilitating condition, recovery involves self-acceptance, awareness of the dangers, and knowledge of the compensating tools. It means a sometimes daily decision to walk in a different direction, a decision to take responsibility for overcoming the barriers that hold us back.

In the fall of 1984, when I was 27 years old, I lost an important political-action job with a progressive nonprofit organization in Washington, D.C. Two months later—while I was still unemployed —my wife asked me to leave, saying that a temporary separation might save our marriage. The way in which these two incidents were handled, more than the end results, shattered my idealism about both institutions; and I soon lost my faith in a third: organized religion.

After finding a small apartment in the city, I joined a weekly Bible study group associated with the church my wife and I attended. One evening that winter I shared, with great awkwardness, that I was contemplating suicide and would appreciate their prayers. Yet, during the following week no one from the group called to see how I was doing or to offer support.

I got through the "deadly February" blues, but I never went back to the group. Or to that church. My wife and I got back together, but five more years of moving, career changes, and not assuming the best about each other took its toll. This time I was the one who took the initiative to move out. It was an extremely painful and confusing time, but I came to look back on it as one of the clearest right choices I'd ever made and I've never regretted it. Still, marriage is mostly a reflection of yourself and I had to take myself with me.

When I lost the first woman I had loved after my divorce, I didn't have the energy to pick up the pieces again. It felt like someone had died. I had read such scenes in stories, seen them in movies—the awkward emptiness, the profound triviality of everything. I felt stupidly like a psychotherapy anecdote. But then, everything in my life seemed like an analogy, a reenactment. I was never sure what I really felt anymore. Did I really love this woman that much—to be so bereft? I had plenty of things to be depressed about: a nowhere job, overdue bills, the increasing absence of my best friend ever since his first child had been born. I was getting on with my life pretty well, actually, with the exception of a few more shards in the heart. I was certainly used to feeling alone. In fact, it bothered me how easily I adjusted to each new loss, how well I bounced back, but it was the one thing I knew how to do well: checking out. Only this time it didn't take. I was tired of being so good at saying good-bye. And when I touched that cold, slippery wall at the bottom of the darkness, the only person left to say good-bye to was myself.

I began writing suicide poems—a topic that hadn't compelled me since junior high. But the growing weight of shadows within me was no adolescent fascination with the mystique of death. I started thinking about buying a gun.

One day I got off the bus coming home from work and was standing on the sidewalk waiting to cross the street—a busy, fast-moving boulevard. While my mind was wandering elsewhere, my body decided to step out in front of a truck—only for a split second, like those moments when you stand on top of a high overlook and imagine jumping off. You physically feel yourself falling. It is not vertigo, it is a seduction of our senses that fortunately is constrained by fear and by our logical mind. But in that moment, standing there on the street corner, I vividly felt the impulse to throw myself "over the cliff."

It scared the hell out of me. Not the idea of death—I'd been thinking about that for many weeks; but if I was going to do something so profoundly final as killing myself, I didn't want it to happen by accident.

The next day I made an appointment with the mental health department of my insurance provider, a major HMO. I came to the office at the scheduled time and reported to the reception window.

"How can we help you?" the young woman asked.

"I'm here to see a therapist," I said.

"Why do you feel you need therapy?"

I thought this a bit personal for a receptionist to ask, but I told her, "Because I feel suicidal."

"Okay," she said, "If you'll just fill out these forms and bring them back to me when you're done."

I filled out the forms, brought them back, and after a while was ushered into one of the inner offices where a middle-aged woman sat at her desk. She did not get up when I came in, but simply waved toward a chair. "So, why are you here?"

"Because I feel like killing myself."

"How long have you been feeling this way? Have you actually made an attempt, or are you just thinking about it?" Her questions went on in this vein, as if I were there for a routine medical examination or a job interview. She seemed to have no idea how self-conscious I felt or how humiliating this process was for me. "Okay," she said finally, "We'll get you back in here next week to see a therapist."

"I thought that's what I was here for," I said, confused.

"This is just an intake interview," the woman replied.

"And who will my therapist be?" I asked, suspecting already what her answer would be.

"Me," she said.

I paused for a moment, thinking about all the literature I'd read encouraging people to be assertive with their doctors and not to turn over all their decision making to the "experts." Then, for the second time in 48 hours, I took the initiative on my own behalf. "I don't feel comfortable with you," I said. "I'd like to be assigned to someone else."

"Fine," she said.

"And isn't there some medicine or something you can give me in the meantime?"

"You'll have to see a psychiatrist for that."

"I thought that's what I was here for."

"No. You'll have to make a separate appointment, and I don't think there are any more openings today."

She went out to check the schedule. "Can you come back two weeks from tomorrow? That's the first opening we have."

I was stunned. Her curt manner had been bad enough, but this was astounding. What did I have to do, point a gun at my head? Go stand on a tenth floor ledge and threaten to jump off?

"You're kidding," I said. "I just told you that I'm on the verge of killing myself, and you're asking me to take a number—to make an appointment and come back in two weeks? This is not right."

She looked at me. "Wait here," she said and disappeared again.

"Okay," she said, when she came back. "Dr. Zorn can see you at 5:30, if you want to wait."

It was now 3:30. "I can wait," I said. I wasn't expected back at work for the rest of the afternoon. So I waited.

Dr. Zorn (not his real name) ushered me into his office. "So, why did you want to see me today?" he asked, as if I had just dropped in.

"Didn't they tell you?"

"I want to hear it in your own words," he said, and I was forced to explain everything again. Then he wrote me a prescription for Prozac and confirmed that I was coming back next week to see a counselor. Later, I was told that my case had been mishandled, even for an HMO. It was supposed to be mandatory procedure that any patient in my situation be admitted right away to the psychiatric ward of a local hospital. (I don't think I would have wanted that either, but there must have been something in between.)

Dr. Gleason was everything I could have hoped for in a therapist. He was gentle, compassionate, attentive, insightful, willing to share of himself, and willing to be direct with his opinions—not just the clichéd how-do-you-feel-about-that? approach. Unfortunately, my health plan only paid for six therapy sessions.

But it was a start.

Redemption is a process, of course, its beginnings often hard to define. My conversion away from despair involved many subtle moments, and the point of transformation is no less mystical for the deliberate choices required. Several factors brought me back from the brink of suicide: deciding to get therapy, falling in love again, and reading William Styron's *Darkness Visible: A Memoir of Madness*, which recounts his own lifelong struggle with depression.[2]

Styron's short book emphasized two powerful truths that I readily identified with: first, depression is an illness, not laziness or self-

2. William Styron, *Darkness Visible: A Memoir of Madness* (New York: Vintage Books, 1992).

indulgence; second, most people who have not experienced severe depression will never comprehend the weight of it or understand the helplessness behind its symptoms. To have my own experience portrayed so precisely was a liberating acknowledgment. Knowing that I struggled with an affliction common to many people, I could finally let go of the tremendous burden of guilt that always compounds the debilitating effects of depression. And this freed me to focus on those things that I could change.

The decision to seek counseling—admitting that I needed help— was an important step for me. This simple act of taking responsibility for my own fate was probably more significant than anything I learned in therapy. Dr. Gleason did give me a useful tool, however, with the concept of "emotional economics." I learned to look more consciously at what kind of emotional or spiritual payoff I was getting from the things in which I invested my time and energy. When I looked at what I most wanted out of life—an intimate relationship, a sense of community, and a clearly expressed vocation—I realized that my priorities in time and effort were exactly reversed in terms of what brought the greatest return. Writing was the one area that consistently gave me the strongest sense of accomplishment and the clearest affirmation of the best part of me. Yet this was the area in which I invested the least time.

In the next four years I published two books, both of them exploring my childhood. As I began to untangle the various emotional strands of my life, it became clear that much of the disconnectedness I felt had to do with a disconnected past. If I wanted to understand where I had come from, I needed to reconnect with the community that had shaped me. Thus, I began a methodical effort to get back in touch with friends and former teachers from high school and earlier, none of whom I had made contact with for more than seventeen years.

One former classmate, now living in Atlanta, Georgia, asked me who else I'd called. David especially wanted to know about mutual friends living in the Washington, D.C., area.

"Andrew Chelchowski lives up there," David said. "He's a police officer in Alexandria, Virginia. Have you talked to him?" I told him that I'd tried—another friend had already mentioned him—but his phone number was unlisted. And the Alexandria police department had never heard of him. "Andrew got shot up real bad a few years ago," David continued. "And his partner was killed—during a hostage rescue attempt that went bad. Didn't you read about it?"

No, I hadn't. But I remembered another close friend whose death I'd learned of that way.

When I was separated from my first wife, I became friends with a man from the D.C. neighborhood where I'd gotten an apartment. Mozon had survived a crippling construction site fall only to become debilitated by lupus, a painful disease that causes swelling of the veins and internal bleeding. After I moved back in with my wife, out in the suburbs, Mozon and I saw each other less and less frequently. One day I opened the newspaper and read his name in a front-page story. It got mentioned because of some scandal about the ambulance getting lost on the way to his house, after his mother called 911. His mother told me later that she found him in the basement, next to a bucket full of blood that he'd been spitting and throwing up into all night. Mozon didn't call for help when he started hemorrhaging. He let himself die.

David continued talking about Andrew: "The incident got a lot of publicity, all over the country, because local TV cameras on the scene captured the shooting. You know, a cop getting killed is pretty dramatic. I saw it on the news down here."

Suddenly I recalled a news segment I had watched one evening a while back: brief images of a red-brick housing project, the rows of shabby wooden fences along a back alleyway, then the shots. I remembered being stunned by the real death I had just witnessed—not a movie. And right here, on the local news. But it never occurred to me that there was a more personal connection. The incident had been dramatized in a *Reader's Digest* story (February 1990), David said, if I wanted to get the details.

This is what happened. On March 22, 1989, a thirty-three-year-old escapee from a Washington, D.C., halfway house took four hostages in a drug-related dispute. Andrew Chelchowski was on the Special Operations Team that responded. Ninety minutes later, three of the hostages had been released. By this time, over seventy police officers had descended on the Hopkins Court housing project. Snipers took up positions to support the ground team waiting for the outcome of final negotiations.

An hour later the gunman stumbled out the back door of the house, stoked on crack and PCP and holding a sawed-off shotgun to the head of the seventeen-year-old boy whose mother's drug debt had precipitated this deadly standoff. He turned and saw Chelchowski and his partner, Charlie Hill, waiting in the alley. Caught in a standoff, the two officers finally agreed to put their guns down if he would do the same and release the boy. Chelchowski and Hill laid their weapons on the ground, knowing they were covered by the police snipers in a second floor window across the alley. But the convict continued to hold his shotgun against the boy's neck, swinging wildly from side to side as he looked for an escape. Then a sniper's bullet hit him in the back and he went down. As he fell, he turned toward the two officers caught out in the open and fired.

"I looked him in the eyes and knew he was going to shoot me," Andrew would say later. "I felt the force of the first shot as it flew past my head. There's no question in my mind that it was intended for me."

Charlie Hill took the blast full in the face. Chelchowski took the next shot in his legs before a barrage of police gunfire silenced his would-be executioner.

A couple of days after talking to David, I decided I'd try again to reach Andrew. I sat down at the kitchen table after supper and dialed the number David had given me.

It turned out that Andrew's number wasn't unlisted. He lived in a small town an hour south of Alexandria. I listened to the phone ringing at the other end and tried to recapture the sense of connection and camaraderie from our high school years. I had no idea what I was going to say, and when a woman answered the phone I was flustered.

"Hi. Is Andrew, uh, Andrew Chelchowski there?"

"Who is this, please?" she said.

"Paul Seaman—a friend of his from high school. Is this Sherry?"

"Yes."

She paused. "I don't know how to tell you this, but Andrew committed suicide last week."

Everything went still. The telephone, the table, the traffic beyond the window all dropped away as I grappled with the words. It felt as though someone had wrapped their arms tightly around my chest, while someone on the inside was pounding to get out.

I understood at least that my history, my feelings, didn't matter at all in that moment. This was Andrew's wife.

"I'm sorry," I said, with as much dignity as I could muster. "Is there anything I can do?"

Sherry immediately impressed me as a remarkably strong woman. She dealt with her pain by being forthright about the facts involved. What good was there in hiding them? And as we talked, I soon became comfortable enough to ask the obvious-but-forbidden questions.

A neighbor had found him sitting against a tree in the park across the road from his house. A sixteen-year veteran of the Alexandria Police Department with forty-five letters of commendation, my former schoolmate had shot himself in the head.

After the shooting at Hopkins Court, Andrew had still insisted on thinking about other people's needs, not his own. He never talked about his feelings, not even with his wife. He took it as a personal failure that he had been unable to prevent his partner from getting killed, and felt he was letting the Department down by having become incapacitated.

Andrew was on crutches for six months. He refused to leave the house all that time, unable to bear being seen as an invalid. Even later, he used a cane around the house but would never take it outside. "Andy was so good at taking care of other people," Sherry told me—and I could hear the heartbreak and frustration in her voice—"but didn't know how to let someone else take care of him. I felt completely shut out from the wounded man inside of Andy."

In less than a year, Chelchowski was back on restricted duty, doing light duties, desk jobs, coordinating drug busts. As soon as he could, he transferred back to the Vice and Narcotics unit of the K-9 squad. He was given a position in which he didn't have to enter the crime scene until the area had been contained, so he would not be directly involved with any confrontations, wouldn't have to run after a suspect. But Andrew felt useless, felt that the Department had created the position for him.

I understood the demons that can haunt even a good life, the despair that comes from feeling locked out of your own dreams, and the fear of being confined to the mundane, taunted by a false sense of failure and by the inability to control your own destiny. Andrew had become addicted to the prescription medicine he took for the excruciating pain in his legs and was frustrated by this dependence, too.

Yet, many people spoke of him as the most courageous man they knew. After the hostage standoff, when he was shot in the legs, it was questionable whether he would ever be able to walk again. Andrew easily could have signed out with a permanent disability pension, but he refused to give up. He cursed his physical therapists, but he kept going back. In less than three years he had returned to a full-time position with his regular unit.

What went through Andrew's mind over the next nine months, and on that sweltering summer night as he sat under a tree in the park? I was ashamed that I could have come so close to a similar ending when my pain seemed so puny compared to his. Even so, Andrew's death tapped into all the unexpressed grief, all the unfinished business log-jammed inside of me.

In fact, suicide among police officers is common—more than in any other profession except doctors. A *Newsweek* article on the subject reported that "twice as many cops—about 300 annually—die by their own hands as are killed in the line of duty."[3]

As I reread the news clippings I had gathered from the days and weeks after Andrew died, I was struck by how conveniently the hostage incident in March 1989 was used to explain Chelchowski's death: ". . . a sensitive man who may never have gotten over the shooting death of his partner." "Friends remembered his physical struggle to overcome the near-crippling injury and his mental anguish over his partner's death . . . the loss of his partner came to be too great a burden to bear." "However intense his physical pain, it was dwarfed by Andy's emotional anguish. He felt tremendous guilt at having survived. Perhaps he felt shame, too, at having to give up his gun facing a shotgun barrel."

For some people the notion of suicide may be unfathomable, but I

3. William Styron, *Newsweek*, September 26, 1994.

was shaken by Andrew's loss for the opposite reason. And that familiarity made me see the hollowness, the hurried quality, of people's simple explanations.

Just a week before Andrew took his own life, Vincent Foster, friend and legal counsel to then President and Mrs. Clinton, shot himself. There, too—and at much greater length, of course—the media insisted that Foster must have been devastated by some professional failure; that he must have been trapped in some dark scandal for which he felt overwhelming remorse. So it was with great interest, and a very personal connection, that I read William Styron's essay in *Newsweek*, which rebuked the shallowness of these interpretations. Drawing on his own experience with depression—"an interior pain that is all but indescribable"—and knowledge of Foster's emotional and psychic struggles, Styron offered more somber and more enlightening reflections.

The uncomfortable truth is that such tragedies are unnecessary and yet they happen. And we will never fully understand why.

I had felt awkward pressing Sherry, however gently, for the whole story. I now see that such a compulsion is not tacky curiosity, but a coping mechanism. We want the details, not out of some morbid voyeurism, but because suicide provokes a glimpse into that fearful chasm of the unknown. We need something concrete to hang onto; and maybe also, we hope that somehow in the details we will find an answer, an explanation for the incomprehensible. But such a pursuit is only a shadow play of the real story. Many of us—out of a failure of courage or imagination—are content to stop there, at the flickering screen, at the texture of the shroud.

I cover my own pain, I suppose, by attempting to sound profound. It took me three years before I was able to begin to put this account together. I still don't know what to do with that big, unspoken part that's left hanging after I'm all finished trying to honestly express what I feel. I do know that Andrew himself would have had little patience for being fussed over like this.

Sherry Chelchowski told me that the week before Andrew's death she had flown down to Andrew's father's house in Florida for a short vacation. She had gone ahead with her son because Andrew couldn't stand to be around his father. But Michael had talked about how much he wanted to be reconciled with his son and Sherry thought the time had seemed right, that something might happen when Andrew came down for the weekend. Reconciliation requires a certain nakedness of the soul. And in the end, it was perhaps not his demons that proved too much for Andrew Chelchowski, but the fear of letting them go.

Maybe my life is on the verge of a great breakthrough. People have been telling me that as far back as my first wife ten years ago. I'm tired of hearing it. Periods of catharsis can be fragile times. Dashed expectations can be debilitating. Sometimes progress has to be measured in baby steps, and self-discipline simply means recognizing small daily accomplishments, rather than wallowing in the discouragement of long-term goals that remain unmet. There is no medicine that can substitute for community, for the power of empathy. The best therapist I ever had didn't offer me the greatest insights, but gave me a companionship of empathy through my struggles. Talking about the uncomfortable stuff takes its power away—like shining a light into deep shadows: it doesn't make the darkness go away, but it helps you see where you are going. I haven't "arrived," but my footsteps are firmer, now, more confident.

So is my future.

A Prison Guard's Story

Kevin Purcell

As I entered the hotel for a national conference on suicide, a friend came up to me and said, "Here is someone I want you to meet. He is a survivor of a suicide attempt and is a correctional officer." Our brief conversation was most informative, as Kevin Purcell told me about his work in getting prison inmates to talk of their own suicide ideation and in getting help to them through education and intervention. This is his own story, followed by his advice for preventing suicides in prisons.

—JTC

I will always remember the day I attempted to take my own life. It was June 1979. I do not recall why, but my dad asked me if I wanted to go fishing. I agreed to go with a friend of his and four of his buddies. They arrived on a Friday to pick me up at my parents' house.

We all stood around talking before leaving for our destination, Leach Lake in Minnesota. It would take us better than eight hours to get there in a recreational vehicle (RV). Before this trip, I had never been in an RV. It was nothing like taking a trip in a car. Besides its huge size, it had many other luxuries inside: a stove, refrigerator, sleeping quarters, storage areas, and a beer cooler. Just imagine all this under one roof, and mobile too.

Not far into our trip, someone asked me if I wanted a beer. I replied maybe later. Later came in about two hours. One guy had Miller Lite and that's what I decided to drink. When the others noticed that I was drinking Miller Lite, they began teasing him, saying he'd run out of beer first, and when he did, he would not get any one else's beer. I drank not only because everyone else was, but also because I was with strangers, going to a place that I never heard of. I drank because I felt uncomfortable.

My dad's friend in the trip was a paramedic. His name was Rick. I talked to him most because I was soon to begin my training as an emergency medical technician (EMT). This four-month training is a prerequisite to medical school. I was happy he was with us. It helped make the time go a bit faster.

We finally arrived at the lake, and I was sure glad because I was curious about what our "new" home would look like. It was time to get out of the RV and stretch. Then we had to unload our equipment. Our "new" home was a cabin. It looked like something you would see in the movie *Shane*. I mean, it was constructed mostly of wood, except for the chimney. The inside was consistent with the outside appearance. It had hardwood floors, an old stove, a small kitchen, and a fireplace. Despite its appearance, it was good to be there. It was a welcome relief from the four walls of the RV.

I do not believe it was too long before someone asked me if I wanted to join the group to go into town to get some groceries. I said no. Why no? I'm not really sure if I had suicidal thoughts prior to his question, but I know I was not heading to the RV to cook up some grub. I waited until everyone was out of sight. I entered the RV through a side door. Once inside I sat down on a bench that was to my immediate left. After approximately one minute, I closed the windows, turned on the gas, and lay down on the bench where I had been sitting all day. It was not much more than a minute later that I got up again and undid all that I had just done.

What made me get up from the bench? This is the $100,000 question. To this day I do not know what I was or what I was not thinking about. Was I worried about being discovered? Why did I want to take my own life?

I'm the oldest of four. I have one brother and two sisters. I considered myself to be the dark horse of the family. Too vague? I did not feel very connected to my dad, brother, or my two sisters. I felt uneasy about communicating beyond a superficial level. I did feel closer to my mom and it even showed. Unlike my siblings, I worked full-time as an ambulance attendant once I graduated from high school. I also went to a local junior college part-time. My brother and both of my sisters all went to Notre Dame. My feelings of inadequacy began long before this point in my life. When? I had to take lower level English and math. I'm pretty sure it was while I was in high school when I also saw a tutor. I even remember the name of one of the guys who was in my class.

I did not belong with any of the many "groupies" that were common at my high school. I had some male friends (most of them from the neighborhood), but as far as females were concerned, I did nothing more than give some the eye. I attached a lot of meaning to my neighborhood and my friends there. I looked forward to getting home from school on a Friday, so that I could head out to the neighborhood. We did a lot together. We played baseball, football, street hockey (loved that), slept out, went to parties, got drunk, threw eggs at houses, broke into our junior high school, and more.

Thinking back on my teen years, I can say that I was pretty much a maverick. I did things on my own. Not all the time, but enough to justify such a label. On Friday evenings, I would drive around, listening to hard rock music, smoking pot, and going to Burger King. It's funny—even when I was with my friends from the neighborhood, I'd still feel like an outsider. I guess one could call it aloneness or emptiness. Whatever it was, it did not feel too good, but it was always a part of me at the time. I mean inside I felt like I was on the outside looking in. What did I do with this feeling? I medicated it with marijuana and alcohol. If you can't express your feelings verbally, then they'll be expressed behaviorally. Remember, in order to heal you must reveal what you feel.

Earlier in the summer of '79, I was "going out" with a girl from our neighborhood. We actually only went out for four days. I know it's the quality and not the quantity that matters, but I was curious. It was only four days, and I wanted to find out why. I admit that I'm sure it had to do with something I did, or said. I recall asking her brother (who I knew very well) about why she broke up with me. He could not (or would not) offer me any explanation. I'm pretty sure I felt rejected, hurt, sad, and more. I did not like to feel such negative feelings, but they seemed to be the reality of dating. Educators and parents should tell young people that unhappiness after a breakup is not only normal, but temporary, too.

To our youth, I say the following. Your parents not only care about you, but, believe it or not, they want to understand you. We all want to be understood. It is difficult when two involved individuals are not, or cannot, communicate with each other. I know it's not something easy to do, but give your parents and yourself a chance to talk and to listen to each other. If you are unable to talk to your parents about your feeling after a breakup, or other stressful event, I hope that you can talk to someone (peer, clergy, school counselor, or another trusted adult). Remember, feelings are just that. They are not right, or wrong. They belong to you. They are pleasant or unpleasant. They make people feel comfortable or uncomfortable.

My attempt at suicide occurred when I was two months short of my nineteeth birthday. When I was twenty-one, my dad asked me if I wanted to go to therapy. I said no. Even today, I regret not taking his advice. You know parents do that once in a while: give out good advice with their children's interest at heart. The reason for my bringing this up is that if your parents ever ask you if you want to go to therapy, please do me (and yourself) a favor before you say no. Ask yourself this: What would it mean to me if I said yes? It doesn't mean you're crazy, or that something is wrong with you. Sometimes in life there are situations beyond our awareness and capability to handle. It's about learning and growing as a person. It's about gaining insight and understanding into current or past situations. As difficult as this may be to understand, it's not about what others think of you. When it comes down to it, it's all about what you think and how you feel about you.

Did you forget that I started out telling about my fishing trip? I did have a pretty good time. The sun was so hot that the tips of my ears got sunburned. I caught a pretty big fish, a two-and-a-half pound walleye. We arrived back home on Sunday. If I remember correctly, I talked to my parents briefly about that good time, but gave them no indication of what took place in that RV when I was alone.

Much has taken place since that day in June. In the summer of 1984, I started my volunteer work at the Samaritans, a 24-hour adult suicide and depression hotline located in Chicago. Prior to working the phones by yourself, you had to be trained. The purpose was to give potential volunteers a feel for what they would be encountering once they were able to man the phones on their own. The trainers would interact by posing hypothetical scenarios to trigger discussion between trainers and potential trainers. The training lasted a total of nine hours. My tenure lasted twenty-four months.

In the summer of 1987, I started volunteering with Metro-Help. This was also a 24-hour hotline, but it's only for those who are under eighteen. Metro-Help also encompasses the National Runaway switchboard. Not only runaways could call, but throwaways, those in crises, and those who needed a referral. If I recall, the training lasted longer and was more intense. It was spread over a two-week period. We met twice a week, for a total of six hours a week. We even role-played and this was really beneficial to the potential volunteer. My tenure there lasted about twenty-seven months.

Thinking back on these volunteer days, I would like to say the following. It was not only an opportunity for me to meet new people, but to work alongside them, collaborate, and aim for a common goal. Whether people are in a crisis period or not, they still think, feel, judge, believe, aspire, and esteem just like you and me. Volunteering is something that you should consider doing at some point in your life. It is never too late to volunteer. It's a temporary collaboration, but one that only the caller and the "liner" can give true meaning to.

In October of 1986, I became a member of the American Association of Suicidology (AAS). I found out about AAS from a friend that I worked with in 1983. I attended the twenty-fifth-year conference in Chicago. In 1995 I became a member of the prevention division so that I could attend those meetings at the annual conferences.

In 1998 I became a member of the Light For Life Foundation, a proactive youth suicide prevention program. I'm also a member of the Suicide Prevention Advocacy Network (SPAN). This organization is committed to developing and implementing a national suicide prevention strategy that is proven and effective, and has worked ceaselessly toward that goal since 1996. Finally in December of 2000, I was asked to become a part of a task force that is going to look at suicides in correctional settings.

Since 1990 I have given about twelve presentations on suicide. In the presentations, I cover facts, myths, triggers, clues, do's and don'ts of prevention, and referral information. I give most of these presentations at the jail. The rest have been in my neighborhood, schools, and a downstate prison. The one presentation that I gave at my local library in 1997 was my first in a community setting. Only three people showed up. Go figure.

In 1992 I went back to school. I attended a local university. It felt strange—I had been out of school about nine years and now I had to find my study habits again. I majored in psychology. In 1994 I enrolled at another local university, a commuter campus. I switched my major to social work and my minor to psychology. It has not been easy. I work full-time and I'm raising three boys. My wife has been a very strong pillar during my life and my schooling. Now I'm a senior and hope to finish my undergraduate work in December 2001. After this will come graduate school. Once I finish with graduate school, my plans at this time are uncertain, although I plan to continue my efforts in suicide prevention.

Since 1993 I have been volunteering at an area high school during their suicide awareness week. I got started by calling the three area high schools to inquire if they had a suicide awareness program. I told them who I was and what I would like to do. Only one school psychologist, Jay, called me back. I met with him in November of '93, and for the most part the rest is history.

The program lasts two days and involves freshman and transfer students. On the first day, the students see a movie; then a professional, usually a psychologist, holds a Q-and-A session and does some lecturing. On the second day, the program continues in the students' math classes. It is here that the crisis workers, the psychologist, and I discuss true and false "facts" about suicide, take questions about the movie, and answer any questions about suicide and depression. A district psychologist started the program in 1986 after a student took his own life at home.

I'm pretty sure it was 1996 when I told a class about my attempt. Jay afterwards told me that he thought I had taken a chance. I agreed, but prior to this another counselor told me about a student who had confessed that she had attempted to take her own life. She was relieved to hear about mine. Since 1998 I have made a point to do this and I have never heard a complaint. I focus on the "what" and not the "how": what has happened since my attempt and not how I attempted. If we make a point not to put ourselves out there revealing personal bits of information, then how can we expect to grow as individuals? This is my story and my truth.

Jail Suicide Prevention

One of the most important factors in preventing suicide among the incarcerated population is changing the attitudes of the officers. This includes, but is not limited to, getting rid of stereotypes, beliefs, and preconceived notions. A second key component is training the medical staff, mental health workers, and correctional officers. Specifically, we need to train them to recognize, respond, and refer a suicidal inmate. By recognize, I mean teaching them about the warning signs. These warning signs or clues can be verbal and nonverbal. The verbal signs can be further divided into direct and indirect references. These references can be, but are not limited to, suicide, death, or hopelessness. The indirect verbal signs are not as detectable as direct signs, but are just as important in assessing risk. By respond, I mean in a nonjudgmental, caring, and empathic manner. Treat others like you would want to be treated. By refer, I mean the following. Refer them to a mental health worker who is available in the jail/prison. Obviously not all jails/prisons have such a luxury, especially after normal business hours or on weekends. In such cases, measures should be taken to assure proper assessment of that inmate through a local hospital or even an area mental health center.

Make mandatory for all incoming recruits a suicide awareness/prevention class. This class should include, but should not be limited to, factual information, risk factors, triggers, proper identification, referral procedures, do's and don'ts of prevention, postprevention procedures, and what a jail/prison could contribute to suicidal behavior. This class should be no less than eight hours. A refresher course should be given at least every other year and should be four hours in length. Supervisors should attend this class, too. In my opinion, officers should pay particular attention to inmates after they return from court and from using the phone. It should not be beneath any officer to inquire about the inmates' emotional well-being following use of the phone.

I believe seasoned officers should receive this training, too. I realize there might be some resistance to such training because recruits are typically younger and more open-minded than their older counterparts. Some seasoned officers have the attitude (at least that is the impression they give off) that, after a suicide, there is one less inmate to feed. Do you understand why I feel it is important to change such negative attitudes? Any suicide prevention program should be fully supported by the administration, and policies and procedures should be in place. It is much more common today than it was twenty years ago for the victims to file a suicide-related lawsuit.

After all successful suicides the officer(s), medical staff, and the mental health staff should discuss decisions, emotions, and any frustrations that arose from such a traumatic incident. I'm not sure how comfortable I am with using inmates as gatekeepers. Let's be real here. Sentenced or not, they have enough to be distracted with. The real gatekeepers are the officers, who are responsible for preventing not only self-harm, but escapes, contraband introduction, and physical assaults, and for intervening during a verbal confrontation, and more.

Each jail and prison is unique. What works in one jail/prison may not work in another. When implementing suicide prevention policies and procedures, we must be mindful of the numerous factors present at any jail/prison. But regardless of the design, such programs need to be supported from the top on down.

You can call me, or contact me with any questions, comments, or concerns by e-mailing me: *KE-Purcell@neiu.edu*

My Last Suicide

Susan Silverman

I met Susan Silverman while she was an associate with the American Association of Suicidology. At the time she was a single woman in her early forties. Her religious background is Jewish. She has since written a poignant introspective account of her therapy and her inner and outer perspectives on one who has sought to take his or her own life. Ms. Silverman's story appeared in the Spring 1999 issue of Surviving Suicide, a publication of the American Association of Suicidology, and is reprinted here with their permission. —JTC

Rabbi Hillel's oft-quoted Talmudic aphorism: "If not for myself, who then? And not being for myself, what am I? And if not now, when?" Each day I struggle to find my own answers to these questions, to live a life of understanding and inner peace, for I am a survivor of my own suicide attempts.

The first time I wanted to commit suicide I was ten years old. I practiced hanging myself from my bed. I was so desperate, lonely, and afraid. I hid my feelings from everyone. It was at this time I began to create a complex set of defense mechanisms to protect myself from being hurt by others. I learned to hide my true emotions and isolated the internal pain, fear, and conflict I was experiencing.

My first attempt came at age 22. I believed there was nothing wrong with me. I quit therapy, feeling that I was getting nowhere. I returned to work immediately, ignoring and burying all the emotions that had led me to my attempt. At age 37, all of those feelings and emotions that I had buried erupted. This attempt at suicide was so serious that I was placed in an intensive care unit for a period of time. I did not know what my fate would be. At the time I attempted, I believed that death was the only solution to my pain and grief. When I woke up, I felt anger, frustration, and hatred toward the ER team that had saved me; but most of all, I felt fear because I never thought I would wake up. I didn't want to live, I wanted to die.

Even though I was in intensive outpatient therapy, the realization that I was a lost soul did not surface until two years later. At that time, I overdosed twice within 72 hours. I knew then that I was in deep and real trouble. My therapist and I knew that for me to stay alive, I needed to take some drastic actions. I was killing myself piece by piece. I could not stop the cycle of destruction.

I am very lucky to have such an incredible therapist. Together, over the last three years, we have worked extremely hard at maintaining an alliance and commitment to the process of healing and recovery. While I had to take the first step and risk opening up and sharing my deepest feelings with him, he is with me every step of the way. He challenges me, sticks by me when I am so full of despair that I want to quit, and is persistent in showing me what life can offer. Opening up was not easy for me because I had never revealed my inner thoughts and feelings to anyone before. Taking that risk allowed me to begin my journey to recovery.

After the last attempt (and in my eyes the final attempt) to take my life, drastic and necessary actions were taken. My parents gave me one of the greatest gifts I have ever received; they sent me to Menninger. Menninger, located in Topeka, Kansas (*www.menninger.edu*), offers adults and children a complete continuum of psychiatric services. I was admitted to Menninger's In-patient Professionals in Crisis Program where a customized treatment plan was developed to address my individual psychiatric needs and issues. The core team of people, in Chicago and Topeka, committed to helping me recover had the difficult task of teaching me to see myself for who I really am. They helped me gain new insights and perspectives about myself. They showed me how important my life is. I still struggle with the painful past, the perilous present, and the unknown future; but, I have learned to take it one day at a time. I now know that I am not alone. There are other people who struggle with the same deep and dark emotions that I feel.

I used to wish that someone could read my mind. For the majority of my life I was crying out for help on the inside, but gave no signals to anyone that I was in serious trouble. I could not let anyone see or get to know the "real me" because I feared they would abandon or reject me. It was easier to play the game; no one would see how much I was hurting inside. I lived a life of secrets. I compartmentalized my life so no two people would know what was happening in my daily reality. It was sometimes easier to live with the secrets than ask for help. Finally, after many, many years, I have begun to learn how to ask for help.

It is not easy to make the commitment to yourself and learn about the miracle of life when you can't even get out of bed. Even though I have made a commitment, I still backslide. My emotions still swing from thinking everything will turn out all right to I can't do this, it's just too hard.

Still, I make the effort to go forward. If I miss an appointment without giving prior notice to my therapist and if I do not answer the telephone within a certain time period (which in the past was quite often), he calls the police. At first, this infuriated me. I now understand that he does this because he cares enough about me to make sure I am alive and safe. Now, I never miss an appointment, even if I am at my lowest and darkest point.

Finding people who care about what happens to me has allowed me to begin to see the wonders and talents that I possess. My parents and friends who supported, and continue to support, me have found how difficult it can be at times to stand by someone you care about. For their continuing support, they have my eternal gratitude and love.

It is my hope and wish that every person contemplating taking his or her life take that first step as I did. Reach out to someone you can truly trust (a parent, a mental health provider, your physician, your religious leader, a trusted teacher). Realize that you are not alone. Take the risk. It is difficult and painful, but people who care about you will be there through the good times and the bad times. They can and will make a difference in your life. Like so many things, I learned this truth late in life.

I am still in the healing and understanding process, but I have equipped myself with new skills and behaviors that help me during the rough and trying times. I have learned so much about myself, and am realizing how different life is since I took the blinders off. I know that my dark and troubling thoughts will not end tomorrow. I also know that, in time, my desire to take my life will diminish to a point where I will be able to deal with the self-destructive urge in a positive and meaningful manner. I have been very focused on eliminating the emotional roadblocks that I had created throughout my life, and there are still many unknowns in my life. My continuing journey will be rigorous and intense. I know that I can and will rise to the challenges facing me.

So to my parents who have struggled with every day of my life, to my team of therapists Dan, Kay, Marian, and Dr. F., and to my dear friends, thank you for caring enough about me to help me find my way and myself. You taught me that I am a survivor of the highest caliber.

My Guiding Star: My Most Difficult Journey

Adelheid L. Weber

Heidi Weber has been a friend of our family for over twenty-five years. Her story is one of unusual suffering and courage, beginning with the death of her mother in an American bombing raid over her native Germany. Her attempt came after her son and daughter were grown, and her achievements since in education, business, community service, and the enjoyment of life are truly remarkable. This is an account of how she felt before she made the attempt on her life and her struggles and joys since. —JTC

As I gazed into the night sky, I was sure that the brightest star was where my mother watched over me. She had been killed in a bombing raid on December 12, 1944. She was visiting my father with my three youngest sisters, trying to get a travel pass back to me and her other four children. Only military troops were allowed to travel without a pass. But the bombs fell that afternoon, before she could start her journey back to us.

I was just ten years old. The war was slowly coming to an end, and there was chaos everywhere as we fled from Waldenburg, now part of Poland, through Czechoslovakia into Bavaria. We could not stay in Czechoslovakia because the Czech people were rising up against the German occupation and threatening to kill every German—including the children.

For many nights afterwards, throughout my teenage years, I hoped that my mother would communicate to me from that brightest star. Somehow I felt comforted just by looking into the evening sky. My three brothers and five sisters were good companions, but no one could replace my mother.

After the war ended, my father remarried. My stepmother tried to provide food and clothing for all of us, an overwhelming task with food so scarce and the stores almost empty. She did the best job she could.

My stepmother had been drafted into the war as a nurse and worked in the Balkan area, seeing soldiers wounded, young men dying. At the end, under Russian occupation, she was a prisoner of war. When she returned, her nerves were so frazzled that her patience was not great with little children like us. But children do not understand these things, and tension was very great at times. My father tried to keep the family together somehow while still being a good pastor to his congregation.

All through my teenage years, my self-esteem was low. It did not help that my stepmother called us dumb and stupid and good-for-nothing. Later, when I studied nursing, my fellow nurses called me "the pious one." When another young nurse and I went dancing one afternoon at a café, she danced all the time, but no one asked me. On the surface, I was glad because I did not know how to dance and felt unworthy of such innocent pleasure. My father felt that all his daughters should become deaconesses, Protestant nuns who devote their lives to serving others as nurses. Four of his eight daughters did become nurses. We were not allowed to wear pants or makeup, or curl our hair like the other girls.

My two stepsisters were allowed to go to the university. But we others did not need to study, our parents thought. We would marry and be taken care of by our husbands.

My secret dream was to become either a midwife or a physician, but I knew that was impossible. My father would not give his permission. My second love was flowers, but when I asked my father whether I could become an apprentice at a flower nursery to study botany and tropical flowers, he said that since he could not provide me with a building to set up a nursery, such a trade was out of the question. I could become a hospital nurse, nothing else.

This was my upbringing. Men were to become scholars, women to tend the house, children, and church. There was no exchange of ideas at the dinner table, and proper behavior was always expected. My school report cards noted that I was "polite, courteous, and humble." And a physician in the hospital where I worked as a nurse asked my superior, "Why does this nurse always lower her head when she passes me?" I did it because I was so in awe of his education.

One incident in school stays in my mind very clearly. When I gave answers to the teacher, I spoke too softly. He could not understand me well. In order to cure that, he sent me into the schoolyard and made me yell the answers up to the class. I was humiliated, but I had to come back into the classroom where all my classmates grinned at me. I will never forget that, I was only eleven years old.

This was at the end of World War II. One day all Germans were proudly saying, "Heil Hitler." Then, practically the next day, they were denouncing him. My belief in the adults was thoroughly shaken. How could they be this hypocritical? I was born under Hitler; for eleven years I grew up under him. During that time, no one ever had said a bad word about Hitler. How could adults change their minds overnight? From then on, because politics were never mentioned in my home, I distrusted adults. I had already experienced the loss of my mother, the loss of all our belongings, and the loss of a stable home. We had been sent from place to place, been shot at during the trip from Czechoslovakia and when fleeing from Russians and Poles. We had been through bombing raids, had a bomb crater in the backyard, and felt our house shaking and glass flying. After all that, now the adults had turned around and were saying totally the opposite of what I had always been told as a child.

In all of this confusion came the war trial. I did not understand much about things but I knew something: *We Germans were terribly guilty before God and mankind.* Then I remembered the verses of the Bible that told us how God will punish those who do evil unto the third and fourth generation, but will bless those who do good to the thousandth generation. That meant I was doomed no matter what I did. I asked for forgiveness and I do not know whether I will ever be forgiven for such evil. Even today, I sometimes feel guilt for the wrongdoings of the German nation. For the next fifty years, I could not read or look at anything connected to World War II.

Friends introduced me to my future husband, an American studying theology in Germany. He was a very nice person whom I admired very much. His self-confidence made me trust him. Eventually I followed him to the United States.

My English was very poor, and I was overwhelmed when I first came to this country. It took me a long time and a lot of courage to overcome it. Through a job as a waitress I became brave enough to meet people. Slowly, I was sure enough of myself to converse with my neighbors. But even now it is hard for me to express myself with strangers or in crowds. I still look up to the sky to the brightest star and ask my mother if I am doing all right.

So my early time here in the United States was very difficult. I was isolated because of the language. What I did not realize then, but was told thirty-eight years later, was that my husband tended to keep people away from me, supposedly because my experiences as a child during the war made it hard for me to handle meeting other people. He even tried to break away from his former friends when he noticed I was becoming close to their wives.

After I became seriously ill, he kept people away because I was too ill and could not interact with people. I was too unstable psychologically. Even more hurtful is that my children have told me that he portrayed me as so weak that they should never come to me with their problems. Their own mother could not handle their problems. Was he so jealous that he could not bear to share his love for me with anyone else? I will never know.

When I came to America, not even my education was enough. I was told that I had to go back to high school and pass the High School Equivalency test. My German nursing education qualified me only for being a nanny here. This I did not understand since I had been trained in adult nursing and not in pediatrics, but the evaluation did not seem to take this into account.

For years I struggled, first to get a high school degree, then many years later, to get a college degree. Nine years later I succeeded. When I wanted to start graduate school in biology or biochemistry, my husband told me that I was not smart enough to go on to an advanced degree. Was he afraid I would become too independent with more education? Was he afraid I would not love him anymore and not look up to him as I had done all those years? I will never know.

Stability was not part of our lives. I know that people in some professions like the military and the ministry are frequently assigned to different places, my husband was always eager to go somewhere else. We moved seventeen times during the first ten years of our marriage. Whenever we had established a home somewhere, hung some curtains, and put our clothes into drawers, we moved again. This was not easy for anyone in the family and I tried to make the transition as easy on all of us as possible. Some moves were for short distances, but others were across the ocean to Europe and back again and even there from one country to another. It was not easy to make friends or even get acquainted with people. Sometimes, our moves involved learning another language, or not understanding the dialect spoken in a particular language. I always agreed to the moves because my husband was so educated and I was so ignorant. I always felt like the little village girl, without any confidence. He knew what was best for us.

After moving about the United States, Germany, and Switzerland, we finally settled down in Massachusetts for what I thought would be a long, long time. We bought a house, and moved in. With us, this time, moved a professor of philosophy, a distinguished old gentleman of eighty-four. His wife had died and he wanted to stay with us. I told him that he would never have to move again and could stay with us for the rest of his life.

There were several reasons for asking him to stay with us. His parents had been Jewish. In 1938 he had had to flee Germany. I felt that by doing good to one person whom the Germans had wronged, in some small way I could help make amends for what we had done to the whole Jewish nation. He spoke German, and my children, a boy and a girl, would be exposed to the German language and culture. I personally could learn a lot from him, and practice some of my nursing skills. He offered me some pocket money to take care of him. I thought that this would make me feel I was contributing a little bit to the family budget, since we were very short of money. But his care tied me to the house practically all the time. I could not join the family on trips to the mountains for skiing. We rarely went out for anything. I tried to take care of him, the children, the house, and the garden.

We had some connections to the family of a young girl from Germany who came to help me for a year. This was good because the old gentleman, whose eyesight had gotten bad, dictated a whole book to me that I wrote out in longhand and then typed. It was published later that year. Then, he fell in his room and broke a hip. This made nursing him even more challenging, especially when his daughter accused me of pushing him downstairs to injure him.

During that time, I also began a building project in the house. I built out the attic while my husband was on a trip to Germany. This gave my son more privacy which I hoped he would cherish. It was a big project since I did not have any prior experience in carpentry. All this work was strenuous, but I enjoyed it.

Some time before we moved to Wellesley and after ten years of marriage, my husband began to exhibit a tendency towards bisexuality. It disturbed me a lot, but he told me I must loosen up more and be "with the times." This was a trendy thing to do, he said, and I should enjoy it. I really never did.

It bothered me more than I realized. My bed was being used for things it was not intended to be. What was even worse, it penetrated into our family life and affected our children. They could not say why, because they did not realize what was happening between their parents. I tried to be open and accept what my husband was doing, but it was very hard for me. He told me, "I have the best of both worlds, because I have you and my homosexual friends."

I thought I loved him so much that I could never leave him. That thought never really entered my mind. He told me that he loved me and needed me. I did not realize how dependent I was on him. I knew it in material ways; I did not have an education in the United States. But I was psychologically so dependent on him.

Then came a great blow to my husband's ego. He lost his teaching job. He became depressed and moody. Within a relatively short time, he found another job and we had to move again. We found a house in the new city and bought it. I organized the entire move, selected the moving company, did almost all the packing to hold down the cost, and made sure that the old gentleman and the children were properly taken care of. I also tried to convince my husband that losing his job was not his fault, but part of downsizing and restructuring. He was still depressed and viewed it as a failure in his life.

After the move, during the summer when all the work of moving in and settling had to be done, he went to Switzerland and left me alone with all the work. I hired a young philosophy student from Germany to help me entertain and help with the care of the old gentleman. But it did not work out that way. He was too clumsy to do any housework and the old gentleman did not want him in his room because he thought he was strange.

Later, I found a suicide note on the nightstand of this student. I asked him if he was unhappy and he told me he wanted to go back home after making an extensive trip through the United States. That, he did. Here again, my husband left all the decisions up to me and did not talk to the young man. I was glad when the student left because he made us all uncomfortable. He took the trip and left for home. I never heard from him again.

We had a friend with us during that time, too. He was staying with us and helping wherever he could. While he was staying with us, he became seriously ill. After three serious pancreatic attacks during which he could have died, he finally found a physician who diagnosed his illness correctly. He needed an immediate operation. If he had had another attack, he would not have survived it. I sat with him in the emergency room and waited anxiously. He was operated on successfully, survived, and is well now.

In our new house, another two rooms were needed. I built them with the help of this good friend during my husband's absence. The old gentleman was unhappy because he did not have the physicians he had before. My daughter was unhappy because she had to change school and did not like it at first. My son was unhappy with the piano teacher I got for him.

My husband finally returned from his trip to Europe and things seemed to settle into a routine. Then I started to feel the strain, and my strength seemed to leave me. I felt like an old, old woman. The old gentleman, now eighty-nine years old, had more energy than I had. Every day I was supposed to walk with him and not let him out of my sight in case he should fall. I went with him a little bit, watched him go on, sat under a tree, and cried. I was too weak.

My husband began bringing his "boyfriends" home again. I had to get up nightly with the old gentleman to keep him from wetting the bed. Sometimes he had delusions of wanting to go to the train station to pick up his wife, who had died six years earlier. My ten-year-old daughter became jealous because I spent too much time with the old professor. My fifteen-year-old son simply withdrew from everything.

I fought to stay well but seemed to go down all the time. My moods were getting darker as I lost more strength. Every night my sleep was interrupted. I tried to take care of the family, but I do not know how much I succeeded. Much of that time I've forgotten.

In early spring, two young women came from Austria to help with the household chores since I could not do much anymore. I wandered through the streets, crying, thinking that if someone wanted to take me anywhere, I would follow them like a little puppy dog. If a religious group, no matter what kind, would take me in, I would go to them without hesitation.

"Just let me rest and sleep," I cried. Then the wish became more focused: I wanted to sleep in my mother's arms. How would I get to my mother? She was up on that star, calling me. I could no longer enjoy the early spring flowers; I was too tired. I could no longer hear the birds of spring; I was too tired. Yet I got up every night to help the professor.

I knelt before my husband and begged him to help me by sending the old man away, but he would not do it. Later, he told me he was afraid I would have been angry if he had done so. I do not believe that. He did not want to act because he was too busy with his own sexual adventures and did not want to be disturbed with such things. And where would he have sent him? Later, after it was too late, a solution was found. The old professor was sent to a sanatorium in Switzerland.

In an attempt to end all this turmoil, I took twelve mild sleeping pills, but I told my husband because I was scared. He took me to the hospital and vomiting was induced immediately. The pills did not put me to sleep, but the physician was very angry with me. I was sent to the psychiatric ward where I spent some time in isolation. My husband brought me a red carnation and I ate it because I did not want anyone to take it away from me. I know I did some puzzles there and I still have one of them. I did some other craft projects, little things, and some I still have.

I also begged to have a gynecological examination. For years before I became so depressed, I had bled every day except for about five days a month. Since moving to our new house, I had not taken the time to get a physician for myself. I was just too tired. Now the physician decided on a hysterectomy. So the operation was performed and I was sent home afterwards for recovery.

This was a big mistake. My hormones were out of balance, and I should have been kept in the hospital until the hormone replacement treatment could take effect. I was still so tired that I just wanted to sleep. A psychiatrist was assigned to me, or my husband found me one; I do not know which was the case. I do not know many of the things that happened during that time.

I begged the psychiatrist to put me into a sleeping program where I could be monitored. He told me such things are only done in Russia, not in the United States. He was certainly not the right person for me since he was the doctor who sent me home under the watchful eyes of my husband. But I wanted to sleep. I wanted to sleep in my mother's arms!

I was thirty-nine years old, almost forty. My mother was killed when she was forty and I was ten. Just like my daughter and me. I figured that my daughter would survive just as I had. I was just so tired, I could not go on. My husband had his "boyfriends"; my son was not home much at all.

Then, one late afternoon when I seemed to be better than I had been for a long time, I got angry with my husband for following me around. "Can I not even go to the bathroom alone?" That is when I was *alone for a few minutes.* I do not know how I had hidden the pills there and I do not know what I took. But I took an overdose. Then, I went to my children and said good night, I went to bed and asked for some music, probably a Bach cantata.

My husband said, "I'll give you a sleeping pill so you will have a better night's sleep." That is all I remember. I wanted to sleep in my mother's arms; she was on the star and I was going to her.

The next morning, I was unconscious and was taken by ambulance to the nearest hospital. Two dialyses were done, but little hope was given. For days, I hovered between life and death.

Sometimes I wonder if death did occur. I dreamed I was in a funeral home. I was in a lower room on a downstairs floor, dark and gloomy. Above me was the old professor. His comfortable bed was located in a bright and nicely decorated room with all the amenities he needed. He got meals served on a silver platter, with young men serving him and fulfilling his every wish. I was on a very rickety old sofa, without any comfort, alone and awaiting cremation. The furnace was ready for me. I was tossed into the fire. Then I was in Frankfurt, right after a terrible bombing raid with blackened burned-out buildings silhouetted against the darkened sky. Ruins and rubble were all around. I could not see a single human being. Cold! Devastating! Absolute silence.

Suddenly there was a loud thunderous clap, louder than thunder and more terrifying. Moses was standing there, tall and imposing, in a long gown, holding the Ten Commandments and ready for judgment. It was awful. It was dreadful. In great anger, he threw the tablets down with a big crash. He was furious and enraged.

Then, a beautiful, peaceful hill, all covered with white, whiter than snow, with a bright light in the distance, more brilliant than diamonds, so beautiful it cannot be described. Crystal-clear water came running down in the middle of the hill, sparkling and fresh. Peace, peace, peace. Saints walked slowly and majestically toward the light. They were clothed in long robes of pastel colors, just ever so quietly, peaceful and with dignity, they were converging, moving, toward the light.

Later, I was told that my husband had made the sign of the cross on my forehead every time he visited me in the Intensive Care Unit. Once the doctor told him that he should go home, take a valium, and get some sleep because there was no pulse or blood pressure. But the next morning, when he inquired about the time of death, he was told that I had asked for some ice cream. I do not recall any of this.

How long I lay there, I do not know. When I really came to my senses, I looked down at my legs and discovered that one of them was black with toes like little raisins. The leg had to be amputated. I did not entirely grasp what this meant, but I knew that God was punishing me for what I had done to myself. My husband kept telling me after the first suicide attempt that I had called God's wrath upon me and that he would never forgive me. Suicide cannot be forgiven!

Then started the journey back into life, a life of pain and struggle. I had to learn how to stand up again. Weakly, I stood between two bars to make the first steps on one leg. The stump hung loose and lifeless, though pain shot through it as the nerves signaled that they had been severed. I started pulling up the short leg, and it locked into that position. The physical therapist did not like it, she wanted me to straighten out my leg. I could not do it. I still had the knee but that, too, was in locked position close to the body. Many hours of therapy followed. I was taken to the hospital toward the end of March. My husband complained later, "You promised me to be alive for my birthday on March 31." My first short visit home was in June. I stayed home for an hour or a little more for a trial period.

The leg healed very slowly. At one time, the physicians wanted to cut above the knee but gave it a few more days to heal. It helped and did not have to be amputated higher up. A year later, after many trials and my inability to walk on a prosthesis, a new surgery was performed to bevel down the bone to make it less sharp at the end. Then, with the help of crutches, I made slow advances.

One and a half years later, I was able to enroll in the arts program at a local university. This was to be a trial. For several semesters, I took one art class at a time. I wanted and needed the contact with the outside world, to show myself, that, in spite of my handicap, I could function. My husband had been warned while I was unconscious that I would only have the brain capacity of a six-year-old if I regained consciousness. Now I needed to prove to myself and the people around me that I could function normally.

With my children, I had a very halting relationship. My son was not home very much. He had entered high school the fall before and was busy with his friends. I do not know what he was thinking about me. He was courteous and polite, not a rebellious teenager. My daughter and I made a game of my leg, calling it a horsey. She came to me some, but neither brought their friends home. They were too embarrassed about their mother, or so I thought. I did not know that their father had told them not to disturb me or come to me with their problems. Later, my son confessed to me that he did not want to stay home much because he felt that something different was going on in our house and he could not tell what.

My husband wanted to involve me in sexual activities. There were always young men coming and going. But I refused to be used that way anymore.

Eventually, my son left for college. By now, my husband had a steady outside "friend" whom he visited regularly. This friend came also to the house, and the atmosphere was very tense when all three of us were together around the kitchen table. I begged my husband not to bring the friend home, but he would not listen.

In the meantime, I had transferred from arts to biochemistry. In 1979, while working on my degree and after my daughter turned sixteen, I entered the workforce as a technician in a laboratory. I wanted to be sure it was the right field of study for me.

In 1980, while working and attending university, my husband's parents became so ill that they could no longer live alone. Over the New Year, in ice and snow and very dangerous driving conditions, I had to bring my father-in-law to our home from Pittsburgh. My mother-in-law was in the hospital there with pneumonia. Daddy had two broken hips and was unable to walk. I got him and a few basic things, a wheelchair, and his little dog into the car and drove back to our house, an eight-hour drive. My husband was in Europe on important business, making contacts.

During the next three weeks, while my husband was still away, I fixed breakfast for and washed my husband's father, went off to my job, then returned during my lunch hour to fix lunch for him. Three times I found him on the floor. I had to call the rescue squad to get him back into the chair, begging him not to get up again. In the evening, I hurried home to prepare supper for us and then get Daddy into bed. By the time my husband returned, we had found a relatively good routine.

My husband then got his mother and brought her to our house. It was soon apparent that his parents could not stay with us. Mother and son had never gotten along well. With the help of a good friend, my husband found a nice place for them in a well-run Christian nursing home, since Daddy could not walk and Mother needed constant supervision with her drugs and medications. A year later, Daddy died. We all took turns visiting Mother.

Meanwhile, I had developed severe ulcers. I lost 15 pounds and went down to 110 pounds. Over Christmas I was hospitalized, exactly what I needed. Christmas dinner came through a tube into my stomach! But I did not mind, I did not want to be home with my mother-in-law and my husband's boyfriend. I did not want any part of it.

The physician searched for the reason for my severe ulcers. Finally, I asked haltingly, could it be that my husband has a boyfriend? Then the physician exclaimed that he had found the reason for my troubles. He was the same physician who had treated me after my suicide attempt. He hinted that I consider separating from my husband, but I refused.

I still loved my husband so much and was very dependent on him. He had the education and earned much more than I could ever hope to. He needed my support for his lifestyle and told me that, if I did not let him go with his friends and to his friends, he would start hating me. I did not want to be hated. I also knew that I never could tell anyone except the doctor what the real reason for my problems could be. My husband might lose his job, and we could lose everything. I could not risk that for my children's sake. We never had much money, so he would not be able to give me any support. I was still struggling with my walking and in lots of pain. I was still trying to finish my education so I could get a better position and earn more than the minimum wage. My husband knew all that and used it to the fullest in manipulating me. Whether knowingly or out of instinct, I will never know!!!

With rigorous treatment for the ulcers and some counseling, I slowly got better and regained my strength. For years I had gone to the psychiatric clinic in town to find the real reason for my attempted suicide, but it was always the same story: the caring for the old gentleman. I did not want to search any further or deeper and no one could bring out the reason into the open.

Finally in the summer of 1983, I had enough credits to graduate with a bachelor's of science degree. What a proud and happy day it was for me. Nine years of classes were completed successfully. Just before graduation, I was hired for a more challenging government laboratory job in a university environment. I was being recognized for my own work. My English was good, no longer a barrier. My son was married and settled in Wyoming where he changed his field of study from international relations to engineering. It had been a long struggle to reach this goal. I was happy.

The next year, after twenty-seven years in the United States, I decided that it was time to obtain my American citizenship. After filling out the papers and passing a test, I was sworn in as a citizen of the United States on the U.S. frigate *Constellation* with a small group of other new citizens. It was an important day, a beautiful ceremony full of meaning.

In 1985, even though my husband claimed I was not smart enough, I started graduate school in biology and genetics. But I had to cut back on the biology classes when my husband became seriously ill.

In January 1986, after repeated nudging and prodding, my husband finally got tested for AIDS. I had tested negative in October the year before. His test came back positive. He was devastated. From then on, he lost the will to live. Twice he entered the hospital, first for pneumonia, and later to have his blood sugar adjusted. The second time he slipped into a coma from which he never really recovered. His brain had been seriously damaged, and he could no longer hold conversations. His vision was so impaired that he had to be guided everywhere and he got a staphylococcus infection in his arm. I took him home against the physician's advice. I felt that the dignity of dying peacefully was more important than staying alive longer on a life support system.

My daughter was working at that time in a store to earn some money for the fall semester. She cut her hours back a lot and my son came the last two weeks of my husband's life to help with the care. My laboratory allowed me to go home frequently to check on my husband. His colleagues came and supported him, the congregation where he was a minister brought food and kindness. Everyone helped. My husband died on the day I am writing this twelve years ago. May he rest in peace.

After my husband's death, I felt a great need to become involved with other AIDS patients to learn more about the disease and about homosexual men. I became a "buddy" to several men at different times and helped make it easier for them to die. At that time, there was no effective medication available. Working at my job and helping in the evening was then my main task. It helped me through the grieving process. I helped ten young men die more peacefully. Two years later, I volunteered for a program called Border Babies that provides care and adoption services for babies left in the hospital by drug addicts.

Then I was ready to go back to graduate school. This time I decided to concentrate on finance. Three and a half years later, I received a master's degree, again despite the predictions of my husband. In 1991 I received the "Woman of the Year Award" from the American Biographical Institute and became a "Lifetime Deputy Governor." I became a member of the American Management Association and received the "Achievement in the Arts" award of the Washington Performing Arts Society in 1992 for my commitment to the arts. At work, I received my "Service Award to the Government." I also received a "Certificate of Merit" for a major contribution to pesticide analytical chemical analysis and was included in the "5,000 Personalities of the World" for Outstanding Service to the Chemistry Profession. Later that year, I was selected as one of "2,000 Notable American Women" for my achievements and outstanding service to the community, state, and nation, and was included in the *International Who's Who of Intellectuals*, International Biographical Centre, Cambridge, England. In 1993, I was included in *Who's Who Worldwide* and in 1994 was listed in the *Who's Who in American Nursing* of the Society of Nursing Professionals. I became an "Esteemed Member of Sterling Who's Who" for excellence and leadership in their chosen field of endeavor and am now listed in *Who's Who in America*.

My life changed again when a reckless driver drove full speed into my car, seriously injuring my back. I went back to work for a few months, but the pain was intolerable and I had to have back surgery. But I was declared disabled and left the government services to recuperate for several months. Slowly, I started driving again with the help of hand controls and special seating to support and cushion my back.

That summer I bought a recreational vehicle and drove with my dog and two cats across the northern United States, visiting friends and national parks along the way until I reached my daughter in California. I left my animals there, and traveled to Europe to visit all my sisters and brother. I finally was able to tell them about my husband and my life in America. Ten years after his death, I felt I could openly tell them everything. They were angry and could not understand how a man's character could change so much.

When I came back, I continued my trip through the South since it was winter by then. My trip went through all the border towns of Texas with Mexico. What impressions I received! How many friends I visited! It was marvelous! It was a trip over almost a year's time and I will never forget the beauty I saw.

When I came back from that trip, I moved to the small town where I had decided to settle down and buy a small one-bedroom cottage that needed lots of renovation. Over a period of two years, with the help of a carpenter, I drew the floor plans and was the main contractor for the whole building project, transforming the one-bedroom cottage into a beautiful three-bedroom house with provisions for wheelchair accessibility should that become necessary.

Now, I have a cozy home with a landscaped garden and enough room for my dogs to play. My two cats are very content with their new home. I have welcomed many guests in the nice guest quarters I built. I have joined the Horticulture Society and the Bonsai Club, I give regularly to "Habitat for Humanity," and I help out in a flower shop in town. I visit a nursing home about once a month and go to church regularly. I feel part of the community, and my neighbors like to chat over the fence for a brief morning "hello." I am always willing to help them if I can, and they are just as happy to help me.

One of the important lessons I have had to learn, and this was not an easy lesson, is that I must avoid those who do not welcome me into their homes and their lives. In my eagerness to help and give, without knowing it, I have somehow pushed some very dear people away. I know, however, that as long as they are alive, there is hope for reconciliation and understanding.

I am currently working on making photo albums of all the family photographs for my children. I am determined to stay in touch with my many relatives and friends throughout the world. This way I feel happy and needed by people around me and by all the people I love and cherish. It gives me hope and strength in spite of the pain and disabilities that I experience every day.

In the evening, when I look up into the sky, I see the stars shining brightly. I think of my mother, I think of my family and of friends near and far. Often, I wish they could be here with me. They could experience the blessings I have received after all the darkness. I know they love and care for me, looking up into the same sky and the same stars wherever they may be. My mother is still my guiding star.

7

To Hell and Back[1]

Kenneth F. Tullis, M.D., F.A.S.A.M.

Ken and Madge Tullis organized the first Tennessee State Conference on Suicide Prevention, to which I was invited to conduct a workshop on suicide from religious perspectives. Upon learning of Ken's experience, I invited him to speak to the OASSIS-sponsored first National Interfaith Conference on Religion and Suicide. Later, he and Madge initiated the first statement on suicide by the Episcopal Church, approved in the summer of 2000. Ken, a psychiatrist, is medical director of the Dual Diagnosis, Psychological Trauma, and Impaired Professionals Programs at Lakeside Behavioral Health System and a fellow of the American Society of Addiction Medicine. He has worked nationally with SPANUSA (Suicide Prevention Advocacy Network) to implement Surgeon General David Satcher's National Strategy for Suicide Prevention in the United States. —JTC

My life was over. I knew that much.

January 1982, the neurotrauma unit. I came up from the depths, surfacing into a cold gray day. The IV hurt. The short backless hospital gown left my ass flapping in the breeze. My arms and legs were

---

1. Ken Tullis's story is from a forthcoming book he is writing.

like overboiled pasta, flopping helplessly. Nurses came and went. I never looked up, never spoke. What was the point? Why should I do what everyone had always expected of me? I was dead.

And then the thoughts and feelings hit, slamming into me like breakers after a storm. I was *not* dead. I was full of fury at being alive, back from death not once, but twice. I hated that bastard God and knew with all my soul he hated me back, every bit as venomously. But that had nothing on my hatred for myself. Hopelessness choked me like coal smoke—probably the first fumes of the damnation that awaited me, if God-people had it right.

Pain burned deep inside me, searing the inside of my head. It was too intense for tears, for words: it would not be released, and it could not be ignored. Everything *hurt*—life, in particular. If this was living, I wanted out, desperately.

I spent the next few days as a prisoner in Madison Heights,[2] my own hospital. The attendants, there around the clock, might wear white uniforms, but I knew better than that: they were guards. I hated them, too, dumb bastards. Some wanted to preach and pray over me; others pretended nothing had happened. Which was worse? I didn't know; I simply hated them all.

This was death row, and I was both the condemned and the executioner. Every meal seemed my last one, fattening me for the kill. No more appeals, no prospect of a pardon. I had been judge and jury; I had passed judgment upon myself with no scrap of mercy. I thought of Hester Prynne wearing her scarlet A for adultery. I wore a black S for suicide. "At least adultery is an act of living," I thought.

Unit secretary is a one-of-a-kind job on a psychiatric unit, about halfway between mother confessor and traffic controller, with a dash

---

2. Except for Madge, all names of persons, places, and medical facilities have been changed.

of cruise director. Robin was a good one. She cared about her work, but more importantly, she cared about her patients and their doctors —even me. As a doctor, I counted on her to route all the damn paperwork—charts, blood work, orders, consults. Robin would make it all happen, as though by magic.

I knew enough to believe in her, even if I could not believe in me. I trusted her, and I respected her opinion. She, of all people, could assess the psychiatrists like a Kennel Club judge at a dog show. If she thought well of me, that would carry some weight. And so, when the nurse's voice squawked through the white-box intercom strapped to my metal bed, "A 'Robin' to see you," something inside me yearned for her presence, as a prisoner on death row might want to see the chaplain.

She came slowly, softly, to the side of my bed. Her eyes were full of tears, and pain drew lines across her forehead. She took my hand, very gently, and looked into my eyes. I could not resist that quiet look. I felt full of shame and yet oddly safe. I had no words, no explanations, and she asked for none. No bullshit, no small talk, no social "I'm fine," because I wasn't fine and Robin and everyone else in the hospital knew it.

"Ken Tullis, I care about you," she said. Her voice was firm and compassionate, and I believed her—who knows why? "*We* care about you." I believed her again, without needing to know who "we" were. I'd been a practicing psychiatrist for seven years: I can judge tears, laughter, frowns, smiles, blankness, pain lines, you name it. Facial expressions and body language are my stock in trade. I knew she was for real. "Why don't you let us help you?" she whispered, her eyes brimming.

At that moment, something inside me unknotted, and warmth flowed back from my chest to my cold, hurting head. I felt my eyes grow moist and a tear rolled down the side of my face—a tear of peace.

My way almost got me killed, twice. My way got me back in this hospital two times, almost dead. What have I got to lose? Why not let them help?

I rolled my wheelchair through the 8 Calvin psych unit door, the same door I had locked and unlocked for seven years, on my rounds to see my patients. The door clicked and locked behind me. I had no key. It didn't matter. I was home.

The Dilantin and phenobarbital I'd taken in my overdose left me horribly uncoordinated. I overshot whenever I reached for anything. I couldn't walk; I couldn't use a knife and fork. I couldn't take a person's hand and shake it. For someone who'd been the Randall College Ping Pong champion for two years running, this was extremely scary: neuromuscular meltdown, oh no . . . "No way I'm going to live like this," I promised myself as I deftly aimed a spoonful of food two inches to the right of my mouth. If this was life, I'd sooner not, thank you.

Suicide was alive and well within me. Next time, I wouldn't fail.

I've never been a gun person; I preferred drug overdoses and hangings. But, now, guns looked promising. End of barrel in the mouth, reach for the trigger, blam! It's over. I had run this scenario through my head over and over in the past, always stopping short. I hadn't the guts to use the gun. Now I was finding the guts. No fear: just rage, raw and powerful. "Blow your head off," said the executioner, exultant and terrified. I hated who I had become.

God catches you in the strangest places . . . Three feet from the nurses' station, for example. I must have crossed that same spot thousands of times in the last seven years. Now I call it my God Spot. It wasn't a voice, merely something between a feeling and a thought. Sometimes the solution to a problem pops into your mind, effortlessly, after what seems like an endless struggle. It feels like the tumblers of a lock clicking into alignment and the lock opening.

Something becomes possible that had not been possible before, however hard you'd worked at it. It was like that.

Two overdoses. Two best shots at suicide. I should be dead, but I'm not.

Abruptly I saw God, patiently and painfully watching me, staying with me, protecting me from each overdose. God just being present, not hating me, but suffering with me. God *wanting* my wellness and fullness of life, holding back, waiting for me to choose.

I didn't create myself. And I'm not in charge of when I die.

I kept it to myself at first, this knowledge, not sharing it with anyone. But in that single moment, something in me changed.

I left Memphis, heading for Houston and the Woodlawn Psychiatric Hospital, on January 24th. At the airport, I met the eyes of my three beautiful children, who were there to see me off. I had chosen, eighteen days before, to leave them by killing myself. Now, seeing them clearly, I felt a sudden pang of connection, a deep sadness for what I had put them through. I didn't want to leave them ever, but now I had to go, for their sakes and my own.

My wife, Madge, wasn't at the airport. She had done her bit to save me: now she was back in her childhood home, Shreveport. How could I blame her?

My father was with me on the flight to Houston. I had my last drink on the plane, a double gin martini. It felt like the last drink given a condemned man on his way to execution—and in fact it was. For a new man to have life, the old man had to die.

White House of Woodlawn Psychiatric Hospital was built in 1919. It sits out front, while behind it sprawl one-story red-brick buildings on grounds spotted with old trees. South Unit, the newest, is farthest back on the campus. Walking from White House to South Unit with a guard at my side took forever. All I could feel was fear: *Will I ever leave this place? Who's behind those locked doors? I don't know anyone here!*

I was on suicide watch. This time, I couldn't flee into the safe darkness. They'd left me no way to kill myself. I had to surrender all vestiges of my dignity—belt, keys, anything sharp. I ate with plastic utensils handed out, one meal at a time, by a tech stationed five feet from the dining table. And there was Nurse Rhoda, my very own daytime nightmare. She was one tough lady, and I hated her. I thought bitter and scandalous things about her, as I struggled down the hall holding my pants up with my hands.

At night, I couldn't sleep. I felt as though reality was closing in around me like a cloud of biting insects: I slapped them away, but they would not leave me in peace. I slipped into a sort of oblivion now and then, but spent what felt like eternity, night after night, staring into my own soul with a depth of self-loathing I cannot describe, until darkness closed over me.

And then it was morning, and morning was *hell*. Floods of awareness, and awareness meant reality, and reality sucked. I scanned my tiny room, looking for some exit, any way out of this; some rope of hope to hang myself with. Nothing. Suicide would have to wait.

Suicide watch ended, weeks later, with the ceremonial return of my belt. What a relief! Now at least I wouldn't have to hang onto my pants. I was actually grateful for something—a feeling I hadn't known for such a long time. And then I got real silverware, a metal knife and fork that didn't bend uselessly against every piece of mystery meat. "This is heaven!" I thought, cutting up my first meal as a free man. Heaven is a metal knife and fork . . . Well, I was starting to learn.

As life started to stir in me, I felt a wriggle of curiosity. Two questions terrified and yet intrigued me. I was afraid to ask them, and even more afraid to answer them, but they kept stirring irrepressibly:

What went so terribly wrong in me? And how did a smart guy like me end up in a place like this?

My first memories are all fearful: hiding under the coffee table in terror and tears during a thunderstorm. Mom was away, and there was only the maid there with me. I think I knew then that the world is not a safe place. Going to Snowden School: now, *that* was *terror*. Such a small word for such a huge fear! First day of second grade: I dug my heels and refused to leave the house. My father, wearing his big hat, walked me into my classroom to meet my new teacher. He left me there and walked out as I screamed—but silently, inside my own head—"Don't leave me!" Something deep inside me froze that day in 1950, and I've spent the rest of my life trying to find some way to thaw that frozen part out.

By grade four, I had started to find both my brain and my feet. I learned that my intelligence could set me free. Getting A's in my classes felt so good; they made my parents smile and earned my teacher's pleasure. Good grades could fill up the cold hole in the middle of me. They made the world safer. "As long as I can make A's, I'll be okay," I whispered to myself. But even so, there was a tiny niggle of doubt—a corner of insufficiency. Mom had told me when I was four that my father had been the smartest student ever in his medical school. Had he made even more A's? I wished she hadn't said that. . . .

By ninth grade, my shaky sense of confidence was just about stabilizing. I could think about the future. I had my course all charted: straight A's through school, med school just over the horizon. My sails were set and the waters ahead looked smooth and easy.

And then, just as the *Titanic* encountered its iceberg, so I encountered Mary Sims Dawson.

Grade 9 Latin. Latin scared me. Pop quizzes scared me. Even B's scared me. The possibility of an F sent cold terror down into my frozen gut. When I saw that big red F on the pop quiz in Latin, it meant not just "Failure," but "Fatal" and "Frozen" as well. There went my ship, torpedoed. So much for med school. So much for winning my parents' approval. So much for trust and confidence and hope.

I have to kill myself. The thought came from nowhere—or rather, it came from my own brain, the brain that had been going to set me free. Now that my brain had let me down, this thought came to rescue me. It consoled me. My sense of terror faded away; the trap opened, letting me go. I was free again. I had an option, a hope, a new course to set sail for, one that I controlled. It was a secret power, one I could hug to myself, and it killed the pain.

Randall College was my coming out, and Madge was my teacher. If I lacked confidence, she had it in abundance. An outgoing girl with a huge smile and a wonderful Shreveport southern drawl, Madge never met a stranger, only friends. For me, it was both love and jealousy at first sight. I hadn't a clue what to make of her. Could she thaw that frozen chuck deep inside me? Or would she rip all the sails of the ship I was sailing toward medical school? I didn't know which to fear more.

My first drink! I was seventeen; it was my cousin's debutante ball in Greenville, Mississippi. Bourbon and coke filled the cold emptiness in my gut—a hole I didn't even know I owned until that night. No more staring at my shoes. No more playing the wallflower, looking out longingly at the dancers twirling in each other's arms. No more pain. Now I had *two* drugs to fix me, booze and suicide, two secrets to hug to myself, two safe places.

Senior year at Randall, carrying a full head of sail: if not all A's, at least a very respectable 3.4 grade-point average. After graduation, Madge and I got married in July 1965. We settled as newlyweds into our first apartment. Madge started teaching, and I started med school.

"Bullfrog" Johnson taught biochemistry. Bullfrog Johnson had taught my father. Second day in school: Bullfrog Johnson raised his head from looking at his roll book. "Tullis?" he said. "Where are you? Are you Frank Tullis's boy?" I put up my hand, slowly. "Yes, sir," I said, and heard my own voice shaking. "Son," Bullfrog Johnson said, looking straight at me over the top of his reading glasses, "you will never beat your dad's record at this school."

There it was, seeming to explode in my head: that big F. I'd failed even before I'd written my first paper or exam, and my failure had been broadcast to all my two hundred classmates on the second day of med school. I froze in shame. *End of med school. I have to kill myself.* I hated Bullfrog Johnson for that. God rest his soul, he was only being tactless. He couldn't understand.

For the next weeks and months, suicidal thoughts roared through my mind like fire through dry grass. I could focus on nothing else. I couldn't study, couldn't think straight. All my dreams had collapsed; the ship had sunk. I was lost in terror, helpless. There was no safety anywhere. I dreamed only of ways to kill myself. I held out for four months before I finally had to give in. I sank on my maiden voyage.

Leaving med school was the ultimate disgrace. Not only was I humiliated, but I had disgraced Madge, my parents, and my family name. As the oldest of three children, I had been the Hero Child, destined for greatness. Now I was finished. The day I quit school, I planned my death by overdose, carefully calculating dosages from my now-unneeded pharmacy textbook. As I worked through the dosages, my sense of dishonor and failure melted away. Humiliation loosened its grip on me, and I could breathe again. A great calmness came over me. I had found an option again. I had some hope.

Teaching Algebra I in high school was fun and kept me out of Vietnam. In school, algebra had been a straight-A sort of safety for me. Teaching it to eighth- and ninth-grade girls felt safe, too, even though I'd never taught anything but Sunday School before. For a while, thoughts of suicide died down to a small flicker at the back of my mind. But the flicker, lit in Latin I, never quite went out.

Back on course, second try: medical school let me break free of home, with Madge at my side. I *could* reach that shore. This time, I'd beat the terror. I ate my way through biochemistry, downing masses of Empirin with codeine #3. "Take that, Bullfrog," I muttered with each pill. I came in first in gross anatomy! I could make the A's I craved. I didn't *need* suicide: I'd be okay. It was false pride, of course, but I didn't figure that out until later.

Our first child, Ken Jr., was born, and I lost my best friend. Madge taught during the day and mothered at night. Now she wasn't *my* mom, but the baby's. So I looked elsewhere for comfort: Julie was cute, Julie was young, and making love to Julie made me feel good. I had three drugs to fix me now: sex, booze, and suicide. All three were powerful, all three were huge secrets. That summer, Dr. Newton taught me cardiology and dry gin martinis. I've forgotten the cardiology, but I can still taste those martinis on a hot night.

Finishing med school almost finished me. When Dean Caldwell called out, "Kenneth F. Tullis, M.D.!" a wave of terror hit me in the gut. I hated every possible medical specialty, eliminating each and every sort of internship and residency. I was adrift again, with no place to call home. For the first time, I realized that I didn't *want* to be a doctor. I'd got my M.D. only because my father had one.

Straight internal medicine internship was pure hell.

I took my first overdose later on in the summer of 1971—only twelve pills, but for me, a huge step forward. Neil Armstrong had nothing on me! This was a new option, a new fix. I was half scared to death and half exhilarated. Above all, I was *hooked.*

As for my profession, there was one specialty that I thought I could manage: psychiatry. "More teacher than doctor," I thought, remembering how fun and safe it felt to teach algebra. "Besides, it might help fix me." This is a hell of a bad reason to become a shrink, but it's also surprisingly common.

Going back to residency in Memphis felt like returning to the scene of a crime. And suicide swept through my mind constantly: a continual fire.

First-year psychiatry resident, 5 North, Bluff City Mental Health Institute. Damn. I'd never been on an inpatient psych unit. I'd never even seen a schizophrenic, much less had to manage one. I shivered in secret fear as the door clicked and locked. Pat, the 3-to-11 tech who was showing me around, looked interesting. Madge was expecting twins in a few months, and I was about to lose my best friend again. I'd sworn off extramarital sex after Julie and was almost shocked to find myself in an affair with Pat after a few months. But again, sex was powerful enough to still the pain in my gut. The two matched up perfectly. And at least, sex helped dampen my urge toward suicide.

Allergies. Snotty, sneezy, stupid, draggy allergies. They don't ever kill you: you just wish they would. I always prayed for something more fatal, or at least more interesting, but God wasn't listening. The headaches were awful—headaches of every sort: little ones, big ones, short ones, long ones, dull ones, pounding ones. "Migraines," I self-diagnosed with fear and excitement. "I'm getting migraines, like my father. Forget Harvard with these babies."

But Darvon fixed the headaches, so I took Darvon—before meals, during meals, after meals, between meals, before Darvons and after Darvons. Darvons kept the headaches at bay and Harvard on the horizon.

Assistant Director of Residency Training, Department of Psychiatry, 1975. Not Harvard, but on the way. Private practice at Madison Heights in the afternoons. A foot in both worlds. Darvon in my pocket and plenty of prescription pads. Harvard still in sight. . . . I had the world by the tail, it seemed.

Good-bye, Pat-the-tech; hello, Natalie-the-shrink—well, I had always thought psychiatry might fix me. . . . For eight years, we were together daily. Not once could I tell her a word about the Darvon in my pocket and the suicidal thoughts burning through my mind. So much for closeness. . . .

Oh, '76 was a banner year: my mother almost died of a massive heart attack, my dad ended up at Woodlawn, on my referral. Darvon, more Darvon, plus Ativan, more Ativan. There weren't enough pills in the world to quiet the growing terror in me.

Friday, August 13, 1976: I left the note of apology on the passenger seat of my red TR7, where Madge and Natalie took turns sitting. I had 5,000 mg of my own Elavil samples, washed down with my mother's favorite, a cold bottle of Coke. It almost worked.

Waking up in the intensive care unit of Madison Heights. They'd had to bring me back several times on the ambulance ride from Brownsville. As I started to surface, so did the despair—and then the rage. A nurse was trying to fix the IV in my right arm. I took a swing at her. I swore and screamed in the safety of my own head, "I'm not supposed to *be* here!" My god had failed me. Death had let me down.

And here I was, branded by my own action: I'd wear this SUICIDE label till the end of my days. For the first time, I realized just where I was and what I'd done. Another thing to be ashamed of, another failure. It burned deep in my mind: my own soul stank with it. I would have to live with this until I died—but I couldn't die.

I spent ten days on 8 Main at Lee Memorial, the crosstown rival nut ward. My time there worked wonders, or so they thought. I said nothing about my fifty pills a day, nor of Natalie, nor of the steady flickering flame at the back of my mind. Of all people, of course I knew the buzzwords, and just how I could feed them back to my shrink: "stress," "depression," "compulsivity," and (his favorite!) "Oedipus complex." Dr. Harris was pleased with me. Freud would have been pleased with me, too. And since they were pleased with me, I was pleased with me, too. Besides, I thought, as I counted my pulse looking for signs of withdrawal, this whole pill and OD business—just a mistake. No big deal. End of discussion.

Three days later, back in my white coat, with the flowing color-coordinated label over the left breast pocket: Kenneth F. Tullis, M.D., I marched confidently through the halls of Madison Heights, making my rounds. I was now dedicated to sniffing out suicide and eradicating it from every floor of the hospital. With fifty pills inside me, no underwear (to ward off the heat rash caused by all those pills), suicide burning brightly at the back of my head, and Natalie at my side, I was the Hero Child. I would, by God, exterminate every symptom of emotional pain that crossed my path.

Rope! Lots of rope! I browsed through the aisles of Simpson Brothers Hardware. There it was, the perfect rope. *Keep cool. Nobody will suspect a thing.* What a rush! What a fix! A new frontier. . . . Knots usually weren't my thing, but with practice between patients and after hours, I got noose tying down to a fine art. In my biofeedback lab, right beneath the 8 Calvin psych ward, there was a handy piece of black drainpipe exposed. That, with a small brown stool, made a perfect gallows. *Obviously I'm all hung up on psychiatry—enjoy that one, Freud,* I thought, surveying my handiwork.

Again and again in the years from '76 to '82, I would go into suicidal trances. Still in my white coat, I would go to 7 Calvin, leave the elevator, turn first right and then left, slip through the back door into room 703, enter the biofeedback lab, slip the noose over my head, and try to kick the stool out from under my own feet. The hangman in me wrestled with the condemned prisoner in me, while the addict in me stood to one side and copped a magnificent high. Four times I came very close. Once, the hangman won, and I came out of my trance on the floor, the stool three feet away, and rope burns on my neck. For a moment, I was healthily terrified. But then the flame steadied and leapt high again.

From then on, I was in a losing battle with my god and lover, Death. Suicide stayed with me every waking moment, at home, at work, on break, whenever. It was only a matter of time.

Wednesday, January 6, 1982. In my own office, Calvin 703, I reached into the top left-hand drawer of my desk. Days before, during rounds, I had found and confiscated a bottle of Dilantin, and phenobarbital from one of my patients, an impulsive young man on 8 Calvin. I had a bottle of booze in my desk as well. I took the two together, read my Bible for awhile, and waited to walk straight into my lover's arms.

So there I was in the winter of '82, off suicide watch at Woodlawn, in Houston, Texas, feeling absurdly grateful for metal cutlery and my belt. Off suicide watch meant off South Unit, and off South Unit meant starting my classes. Off to school again. Some things never change. This time, I had no mom, no dad, no Madge: only a guard—but a friendly guard. I felt childishly happy to have a friend to walk with me to school. I felt . . . safe.

"No grades! This school has no grades! I can't make an F!" I shouted to myself. All I had to do was suit up and show up and I'd be okay. It was a wonderful gift, a blessing. A uniform—I need a uniform. I chose my blue tennis warmups—with underwear, now that I didn't have to worry about heat rash from those fifty pills. Art therapy had taught me that blue was my safe color. And the pants' drawstring waist let me keep my precious belt safe in my own room.

I was still mostly brain-dead from years of pills, sex, and suicide. I was also a very slow learner—"emotionally challenged" they'd call it today. I had to struggle with the most basic insights, learning them the hard way, by direct experience. My wonderful mind was no help at all.

Woodlawn was a "do it, don't think it, enjoy it, don't analyze it" sort of place. The kid in me loved it. The adult side of me hated it and wanted out *now*. In this internal war I was, for the first time, siding with the kid.

Something was also starting to draw me to chapel on Sunday mornings—I didn't know why I couldn't understand what the attraction was. Few other patients came, but still, I kept on going. Was it some old church tape, something bouncing around in my unconscious from childhood? I'd grown up in a church where Sunday morning means Sunday school: that fact had been etched into my mind. Now that the drugs were out of my system, the etching was still there. So I sat in the chapel, obedient as a trained dog, long after the bell had rung.

That Sunday was nothing special—very plain, very ordinary. I'd sat through chapel, my mind as much on the week ahead as it was on the service. I still don't know what happened. I just know that it hit me again: another God-thing, like the brief God-things I'd had on 8 Calvin—but this one was right off the scale.

All these years, I blamed God for deserting me. I was so angry with him—so furious at him. But he was there all along with me. He didn't desert me. I deserted him.

And then the gentle certainty, rising from the depths—a voice of great quietness and love, that I knew was not myself but God speaking: My good child, my dear one. *Thank you for seeing that.*

I'd always seen God as sitting above me in judgment, looking over his glasses in scorn, waiting to take potshots and find fault with everything I did and was. I imagined God raining F's down on me whatever I did, however hard I tried. I saw God as setting up a standard that I could not possibly meet, and judging me against that standard, without kindness or mercy. Now I found a new God, a friend, companionably beside me. And I knew he had been there all along, waiting for me: patient, silent, constant—with faith in me, as I had never had faith in him. He had endured my unfair judgment of *him*, waiting for me to release my blame, my rage. He had sent people to love and minister to me: Rosie, Madge, Robin, even Nurse Rhoda, the guard who walked with me. He had given me such gifts: my beautiful children, my joy in sports, a world of wonder. For a moment, I knew a gratitude so intense it floored me, and I wept.

Maybe some of us turn our lives around 100 percent in a single moment, but I'm not one of them. For me, it had to be two steps forward, one back. I'd left a real mess behind me, and I still had a whole lot to learn.

May 1982, Madge was pissed, *really* pissed. I didn't think that was fair. After all, I wrote at least once a week, even when I didn't want to. Of course, I also wrote to Natalie, who really *understood* me. I still fantasized about shedding wife and kids and setting up a bachelor pad with megawatts of stereo equipment. I poured my heart out to Natalie detailing the horrors of my existence. I made the hospital sound like something out of *One Flew Over the Cuckoo's Nest*, with a dollop of Dante's *Inferno* thrown in for good measure. Natalie poured on sympathy. Madge didn't.

Kevin Johnson—Dr. Bushy-Brows—scared me even more than Mary Sims Dawson and Latin I. He meant *business*—no B.S. allowed! Worse still, he'd treated my father. *I've got my dad's shrink.* I screamed into my pillow, the night before my therapy began.

Kevin didn't appreciate my plan for the bachelor pad. That pissed me off. He wanted to "explore it." Explore it! I wanted to *do* it. *Don't throw this therapy shit at me, doc!* But I locked my anger away, keeping it safe from being seen—or healed. It took me five months to get up enough nerve to admit to him that I was angry at him.

He could use those bushy eyebrows like a marksman uses a rifle. "You know," he said, raising one of them, "I'm not sure you're capable of commitment." Rage roared through me. What about Julie? What about Pat? What about Natalie? *Don't you know who I am?* But I feared that maybe he did know.

Eyebrow #2: ready, aim, fire: "You never really made a commitment to your marriage or to Madge." Direct hit. He was right, dead right, and the knowledge stunned me.

That good-bye letter to Natalie was the first honest and healthy pain I felt at Woodlawn. Oh, I'd done lots of pain before, but there's the pain of sickness and the pain of healing, and this was the first I'd done of the latter persuasion. Still, it hurt like hell, from my toes to my teeth. I was like a kid losing his favorite toy. My whole world fell apart.

Madge came to visit—our first therapeutic visit. We had four hours together, with a guard close by. Within five minutes, we were raging at each other on the tennis court. She almost left me there. *Don't you know who I am?* But I feared that maybe she did know. That same struggle between wanting to be understood and not wanting to be seen with any clarity at all. . . . We came so close that day to breaking our marriage. My life fell apart a little bit more.

On the other hand, life in the puzzle factory was definitely improving. I was starting to gain confidence, starting to feel better. My teachers seemed happy with me. Freud would have been pretty pleased, I imagined. So I was happy with me, too. In therapy with Bushy-Brows one day, I was spouting off cheap insight with great enthusiasm, showing off my Woodlawn-Patient-of-the-Year persona, when he trained his eyebrows on me, sighting for bear again.

"And tell me, Ken: do you plan to do something about your drug addiction before you go back to Memphis?"

Nice technique, I thought approvingly. *At least 9.5. Drug addiction? Me?* I cast my mind back over my time at Woodlawn. Not once had I craved a drug, not even once. *Wrong man. Not me!*

Leaning forward in his chair, eyebrows up, Bushy-Brows moved in closer. "I want you to contact the Impaired Physicians Program here in Houston," he said, looking me straight in the eyes. At once my heart went out to those poor impaired physicians, whom I was clearly called upon to help. They *needed* me. How could I possibly refuse?

In Lynn's car, on my way to my first meeting, I was on pins and needles, waiting to meet the poor doc whom I'd help that night. As we drove, Lynn told me his story—the depressions, the drugs, the divorce, the shock treatments, the agony. Then he leaned toward me, asking in that "I know something you don't know" voice: "Do you know what was wrong with me?"

"No, what?" I said.

"I'm an addict!" he proclaimed.

"No way!" I thought, amazed. "I'm one, too!" At that moment, years of denial melted away like snow under strong sun. *I* was the poor doc who got helped that night. I'd come home.

Paul strolled up to me after that first meeting, a big smile on his face, and thrust out his hand. "Woodlawn," he said with a sort of questioning authority. "Two years ago."

"Yep," I answered, much as I'd announce my alma mater.

"What unit?" he asked.

"South."

"Me, too. What doc?"

"Johnson."

"Me, too. What room?"

"Last one on the left."

"Me, too."

This was giving me goose bumps. I felt as though God had sent me my very own angel that evening.

Fourth step: personal inventory. I didn't want to do it. Paul said, do it. I did it, and the fifth step, too. Dr. Bushy-Brows was starting to make more sense. Affirming the changes in me, he encouraged me to stick with Paul and the doctors' group. I was starting to *like* my therapist. The first time I cried with him, it felt so safe—a warm, fuzzy feeling I'd never experienced before.

Madge and I, meanwhile, took the best step we'd taken in years: we put our marriage on a one-day-at-a-time standing. What freedom! We gave each other the freedom to stay or go each morning. We chose, that first morning, to stay, both of us, and we have made the same choice every morning since.

As denial melted away, each stretch of truth became clearer. I realized that I'd been addicted not just to drugs, but to women, too: for me, mood-altering sex was exactly like mood-altering pills. If I fell back into those two traps, I'd end up killing myself. And then there was work. . . . I realized, sadly, that working at Madison Heights would threaten my sobriety. It was too big a risk. Madge, our son Ken, and my dad—bless them—struggled to dismantle my old office. But with Calvin 703 gone, would I ever be able to work again?

August 10, 1982. It was a long, long struggle, but I faced the reality: it was time to go back out into the world. All I could do was to trust in God to carry me through. "If you think I need another year here on South, I'll do it," I told Dr. Munford on rounds that day, meaning every word of it. He paused, looking at me thoughtfully, and said, "We've set your discharge date. September 10." My heart almost stopped.

Saying good-bye to Woodlawn was almost as painful and terrifying as stepping through those doors and onto suicide watch nine months before. The "I don't want to go!" part of me screamed inside my head, as I'd screamed to stay home from second grade, years ago. But another part of me knew that I had to go, just as I'd had to leave my kids at the airport back in January. To grow, I had to let go and move on.

My final good-bye was to Dr. Munford, who had been my doctor and attending psychiatrist. A G.P.-turned-psychiatrist, he brought common sense, firmness, and great wisdom to his work. I had come to trust and love him deeply, hoping some day to become more the man he was. "Ken," he said in our last moments together, "you will always have us with you." I cried, thinking of E. T. touching Eliot's forehead and saying, "I'll be right here." I had seen that movie five times that summer and wept each time. E. T. had helped me understand so much. Now *my* E. T. was saying good-bye. It hurt like hell.

"I do have one concern for you that I want to share," he went on. I nodded, too close to tears to speak. "I don't think you're finished with your struggle with suicide."

Terror hit me. "*No!*" I screamed inside my head. The flame had been out for months: now it was awake again. Or had it ever really gone out? Driving away from Woodlawn with Madge, I realized that it had been there all along, but burning so low I hadn't noticed it. I'd been distracted, too preoccupied with the Twelve Steps and other new and healthy things to pay it any attention. But every mile we drove left the flame a little stronger. By the time we got to Memphis, it was burning bright and strong.

Steve introduced me to the doctors' group in Memphis and took me under his wing. I started therapy with Tom. But they weren't Paul and Kevin, and Memphis wasn't Houston. I wanted to go home to Woodlawn so badly.

Like Rip van Winkle, I was a stranger in my own home and city.

What could I say to my children? "So sorry I missed your childhoods." Who were these young people I barely knew? Looking back over the wreckage of my life, all I could see was how much I'd lost, or missed, or screwed up. The pain was intense.

Waking up at 5:00 that morning in September 1982, in the same bed I had lain in waiting for death back in 1976, with the shutters closed, I knew. They were back, the thoughts! Suicide roared through my head. I wanted so desperately to hang myself in our attic, or to shoot myself in the mouth, as I'd planned back in January on 8 Calvin. But this time, I refused to take a pill or find a mood-altering woman. If I had to die, I wanted to be sober. I'd worked too hard on those Twelve Steps.

Lying there paralyzed, I faced the worst moment since Woodlawn. *What do I do now, God? I don't want to die. I don't want to live.* What would all those people at Woodlawn tell me? I thought of those groups, the therapy sessions, the doctors' meetings, Paul, Dr. Munford, Bushy-Brows—even E. T. I knew then: *I've got to call Steve.* I think that was the toughest phone call of my entire life.

Later that morning, Steve showed up for breakfast in his blue tennis warmup—"in case you tried to run," he told me later. We talked and ate, and ate and talked. We've been talking and eating for the last eighteen years, now. I have no plans to stop.

In therapy with Tom the next day, I finally opened up. I told him about my suicidal thoughts. Part of me was terrified that he'd lock me up; but at the same time, I secretly hoped he'd send me home to Woodlawn—my place of safety. Instead, he simply listened and loved me. He's been listening and loving me ever since—again, it's been nineteen years, and I have no plans to stop. Just the other day, I told him I was ready to commit to long-term therapy, remembering the time Bushy-Brows confronted me about my inability to commit myself. I miss Bushy-Brows. I can't imagine life without Tom.

For weeks after that morning, things were tough, but I plowed on, one day at a time, feeling the gentle brush of wings as my angels circled around me. I went on working on my Twelve Steps. It isn't a one-time process; you keep discovering them over and over again. I kept giving it what I hoped was my best shot. One day, the Third Step jumped out at me, almost off that page: "Made a decision to turn our will and lives over to the care of God as we understood him." *It's not there. There's nothing in there, not a word in that step, about alcohol, drugs, or mood-altering women.* It hit me right between the eyes. *That says to turn "our will and lives over to God." But I haven't done that.*

Now I could see—see all the way back to that day in Latin I when I, at age fourteen, had had my first thought of suicide. I suddenly understood. *Suicide had been my out.* I had felt unable to face life on life's own terms: well, I could always kill myself. Even at Woodlawn, I had thought, *well, if their Twelve Steps fail me, I can always kill myself.* Suicide had been my escape route, the thought I'd hugged to myself, my secret "out" from life's difficulties.

But the Twelve Steps don't work that way. They don't accommodate holdouts. You can't hold out from God: you can only surrender completely, or not surrender at all. There are no negotiated truces, where you get to hang on to part of your will and give over the parts you don't care so much about. I had to trust completely, as I'd never trusted before. No outs; no cheap and quick solutions. I did not create myself, and I am not in charge of my life and death. That's God's business. Finally, it all made sense.

September 30, 1982. I sat down with my coffee to start my meditation. This time, the difference in my mind-set was astonishing. *No suicidal thoughts.* I couldn't believe it. *Oh, thank You. NO suicidal thoughts!* I had lived for twenty-four years with that flame flickering at the back of my skull, and now it was gone.

I will never fully understand what it was that happened that day—and I don't feel any need to. I accept it as the gift it was, thanking my God day by day. I will live this day as I hope God wants me to, and only *this* day, until God decides that my time on this earth is over.

Love at Its Best

James T. Clemons

Toward the end of her national best-seller, *An Unquiet Mind*, Kay Redfield Jamison devotes one section to "This Medicine, Love."[1]

Kay Jamison is a lover. She loves passionately her parents, her husband, her friends, the universe at home and in its farthest reaches, academia, her work, poetry, music, life, and herself. Those privileged to know her, even casually, are infected not only by her brilliant mind and genial demeanor, but by her contagious compassion for issues that affect people.

She herself is the survivor of a suicide attempt, which she details in her book and frequently speaks of in her lectures across the United States. Her attempt was made while she was a professor of psychiatry at UCLA. It followed months, years, of manic-depressive agony and repeated suicidal ideation and behavior, including the purchase of a gun and several trips to a spot near the ledge of a high stairwell in the hospital where she worked.

In tracing her life since the attempt, she acknowledges as essential ingredients in her salvation and restoration her understanding parents, a self-giving friend who "redefined for me the notion of friendship," and lithium. In that strange incongruity so often accompany-

---

1. *An Unquiet Mind: A Memoir of Moods and Madness*, New York: Knopf, 1999.

ing the moods of madness, it was lithium which she chose for her attempt to take her life.

Not surprisingly, she gives most credit to her psychiatrist who "taught me that the road from suicide to life is cold and colder and colder still, but—with steely effort, the grace of God, and an inevitable break in the weather—that I could make it."

She returned to her normal responsibilities: "Running a clinic, teaching, doing research, and writing books." While these demanding and rewarding tasks were no substitute for love, they "gave some meaning to my badly interrupted life." Even so, she was still "unquestionably raw and unhealed inside."

Then came her decision to spend a sabbatical year in England where "Love, long periods of time to myself, and a marvelous life in London and Oxford gave both my mind and heart the chance to slowly put back together most of that which had been ripped apart." Her description of that year in those incomparable academic and medical settings is a delicious literary repast with exquisite presentation: "it gave me back myself again, gave me back my high hopes of life. And it gave me back my belief in love." In short, "Life had become worth not losing."

Few indeed have received, and given, the kind of love Kay Jamison reveals in her book. Even fewer receive their first copy of *Gray's Anatomy* at age twelve as a treasured gift from loving parents. And no one shares, in the same way, the agony, anger, and angst of her unquiet mind and heart.

Kay Jamison is a lover, but not a naïve romantic. "No amount of love can cure madness or unblacken one's dark moods." A qualified and reliable therapist and effective medication, properly prescribed and precisely taken, are absolute essentials. "But if love is not the cure, it certainly can act as a very strong medicine."

Love, in its many-splendored facets, is not absent in these stories, even though intense feelings of hatred are unleashed—toward spouses, lovers, friends, and even "that bastard God." Here, however, love is not always so obvious as that which God wrapped around Jonah.

Among the last words of An Unquiet Mind are these:

> When I first thought about writing this book, I conceived of it as a book about moods, and an illness of moods, in the context of an individual life. As I have written it, however, it has somehow turned out to be very much a book about love as well: love as sustainer, as renewer, and as protector. After each seeming death within my mind or heart, love has returned to recreate hope and to restore life. It has, at its best, made the inherent sadness of life bearable, and its beauty manifest. It has, inexplicably and savingly, provided not only cloak but lantern for the darker seasons and grimmer weather.

For the survivors of attempts and those who contemplate the act, for those who grieve the loss of a loved one to suicide, and for all who would be about enriching the lives of others who have been and will be touched by suicide, there is an indispensable resource available in this medicine, love.

— — —

Jonah was in the depths. His being asleep in the hold of the ship symbolizes both his emotional and spiritual despair, as the raging sea mirrors his inner turmoil. Unhappy with his lot in life, obviously angry that God had commanded him to do something he was utterly opposed to on cultural and even religious grounds, and possibly guilt-ridden for having rejected God's commission to save the people of Nineveh whom he despised, he nevertheless harbored deep within him a concern for those who were also in danger, even though they did not share his religion and were not his countrymen. In the midst of the life-threatening storm that would destroy the seamen as well as himself, he said, "Take me and throw me into the sea, then the sea will quiet down for you."

In Hebrew scriptures, Saul the king and Abimelec the macho military leader asked their armor bearers to run them through. Much like his forebears, the prophet asked the seamen to end his life. But Jonah's attempt was thwarted, just as it was for those whose stories are recorded here, albeit not quite so dramatically.

Jonah could have used a good therapist, and a good theologian wouldn't have hurt, either. But all he had was God. Fortunately for Jonah, it was one of God's better days, a day for gentle, compassionate understanding and patience, rather than harsh condemnation.

In a model for all preachers, Elie Wiesel weaves the story of Jonah into its liturgical setting in Jewish worship. Each year on Yom Kippur, the holiest of Holy Days, that same story is read in its entirety. David Itkin, conductor of the Arkansas Symphony Orchestra, has recently composed a moving, intriguing tone poem, *Jonah*, which at its premiere a few months ago included intermittent readings by Itkin's father, who for many years has read Jonah in his synagogue on Yom Kippur. It is a day of forgiveness, the day of wiping the slate clean to begin a new year. It is a time of at-one-ment with God and with all other creatures.

Regardless of our religious beliefs, the literary prophet who wrote about the son of Amattai reminds us that we all live in community and that our actions are of consequence to everyone, even those we happen not to like.

This marvelous blend of cultural, political, and ethical commentary from ancient literature affirms that no stigma is to be cast upon anyone who seeks to take her or his own life. God never gave up on Jonah, the rebellious son, nor should we.

At the end of this theological tale—and that, above all, is what it is—God has the last word: *Jonah, do you still not get it? You are my son. I need you, and others need you, too. You are worth far more than you know. Together we can do so much for those in need.*

In a word, we matter. Each of us matters.

Children of Jonah can take courage. Suicide *is* being prevented. Help *is* being given and received. Hope *is* being restored. And there is a growing number of people across the country who understand, who care, who accept, and who are ready to reach out as compassionate friends, ready to enrich the lives of those who have been and will be touched by suicide

RECOMMENDED RESOURCES

Chabot, John A. *A New Lease on Life: Facing the World after a Suicide Attempt*. Minneapolis: Fairview, 1997.

Collins, Judy. *Singing Lessons: A Memoir of Love, Loss, Hope and Healing*. New York: Pocket Books, 1998.

Ellis, Thomas E., and Cory F. Newman. *Choosing to Live: How to Defeat Suicide through Cognitive Therapy*. Oakland, Calif.: New Harbinger, 1996.

Heckler, Richard A. *Waking Up Alive: The Descent, the Suicide Attempt, and the Return to Life*. New York: Ballantine, 1994.

Jamison, Kay Redfield. *An Unquiet Mind: A Memoir of Moods and Madness*. New York: Knopf, 1999.

———. *Night Falls Fast: Understanding Suicide*. New York: Knopf, 1999.

Marcus, Eric. *Why Suicide? Answers to 200 of the Most Frequently Asked Questions about Suicide, Attempted Suicide, and Assisted Suicide*. San Francisco, Calif.: HarperSanFrancisco, 1995.

Quinnett, Paul G. *Counseling Suicidal People: A Therapy of Hope*. Spokane, Wash.: QPR Institute, 2000.

U.S. Department of Health and Human Services. *The Surgeon Gen-*

eral's Call to Action to Prevent Suicide. General Printing Office: Washington, D.C., 1999.

U.S. Department of Health and Human Services. *National Strategy for Suicide Prevention: Goals and Objectives for Action.* General Printing Office: Washington, D.C., 2001.

INDEX

ABOUT OASSIS

OASSIS is a 501c3 organization whose mission is to enrich the lives of those who have been and may be touched by suicide. It seeks to accomplish its mission by working with six major systems: academic institutions, corporations and labor, health care delivery systems including hospitals and homes for children and older adults, law enforcement agencies, the military, and faith based communities.

For more information on activities across the country, board members, publications, resources, and opportunities for services OASSIS might offer, see *www.oassis.org*.